CHARISMATIC RENEWAL AND SOCIAL ACTION:
A DIALOGUE

Other Malines Documents:

*Theological and Pastoral Orientations on the Catholic
   Charismatic Renewal*
Malines Document 1
By Cardinal Léon-Joseph Suenens

Ecumenism and Charismatic Renewal
Theological and Pastoral Orientations
Malines Document 2
by Cardinal Léon-Joseph Suenens

Charismatic Renewal and Social Action: A Dialogue

Cardinal Léon-Joseph Suenens

Dom Helder Camara

Malines Document 3

SERVANT BOOKS
Ann Arbor, Michigan

Published by Servant Books
    P.O. Box 8617
    Ann Arbor, Michigan 48107

Front Cover Credit: Photograph taken in Brazil, courtesy of H. Armstrong
Roberts.

ISBN 0-89283-074-3

Printed in the United States of America

CONTENTS

PREFACE

A brief historical note on how I first met Dom Helder Camara in October 1962, when Vatican Council II had just opened.

At the time I did not know Dom Helder personally, although he had prefaced the Portuguese translation of my book *The Gospel to Every Creature*.

He came to see me in the Via Aurelia, where I was staying with the Christian Brothers, and at our very first meeting he told me, with the lively imagination of the poet and the passionate ardor of the apostle, how he envisaged the closing of the Council. He described to me in detail the setting of the closing ceremony according to his vision: a hectic, tense anticipation, to be televized to the whole world. The occasion would not be confined to the promulgation of texts, but the conclusions of the conciliar renewal would be presented in a series of striking close-ups: for example, a few symbolic gestures of spectacular ecumenical reconciliation. The world would see the Pope giving the kiss of peace to Athenagoras, to Visser't Hooft, Secretary General of the World Council of Churches, to the Chief Rabbi. Everything was foreseen, even the music accompanying the scenes, and for the finale he kept Schubert's Unfinished Symphony. Helder the poet had planned everything to the last detail.

Since that first, memorable and prophetic meeting, we have frequently spoken together of the Church of our dreams, and at times we have combined our efforts in certain initiatives.

John XXIII had personally distributed the preparatory

1

schemas among the seven members of the Council's Central Committee and had charged me to act as rapporteur for the two key schemas, which in their final stages were to become the Dogmatic Constitution on the Church (*Lumen Gentium*) and the Pastoral Constitution on the Church in the Modern World (*Gaudium et Spes*).

From the very beginning of the proceedings, I was haunted by the image of Latin America, which I saw as the laboratory where the whole question of pastoral care should be reviewed if the Church of that continent—the home of one third of the world's Catholics—was to gain its full human stature. Latin America also haunted me because of its many problems of population and poverty, inevitably resting on the birthrate problem. All these questions we discussed together and, as everyone is now aware, Helder Camara's discreet and effective influence with the members of CELAM (Council of the Latin American Episcopate), of which he was Secretary General, earned us, on more than one occasion during the Council, the support of numerous Latin American bishops, who voted with us North European bishops in our endeavor to get out of certain ruts of the past.

According to the ancients, the dictum "idem velle et idem nolle"—"to desire and reject the same things"—underlies all true friendship. Dom Helder and I felt that by expressing ourselves together, in this book, about two emphases responsible today for a false distinction among Christians—the "socially committed" and the "charismatics"—we might perhaps help them to overcome certain impoverishing blind spots and to cement "what God has united": the first and the second commandment.

In our view, a Christian who is not charismatic—in the full sense of the word, that is to say, open to the Spirit and docile to his promptings—is a Christian forgetful of his baptism. On the other hand, a Christian who is not "socially committed" is a truncated Christian who disregards the gospel's commandments.

We felt that the simplest way of working together — in musical terms, we might say playing a kind of duet — would be for each of us in turn to explain how he envisages the Christian of our time: at once wholly open to God and totally dedicated to the service of mankind.

So each of us will bring to his exposition those experiences that have shaped his past, his life, his own suffering, which is sometimes the sadness of being misconstrued.

Helder Camara is known throughout the world as "the voice of those who have no voice": This entitles him to speak loud and clear, in a personal and vibrant style, and, as we know, he never flinches from the risks involved. Once, when he was opening a conference in Brussels, I heard him say, "Bear with me, I don't speak French, I don't speak Flemish, I speak 'Camara', which means," he humorously added, "that I speak with my arms, my hands, my body, and with all my heart."

In the following pages, it is the bishop of the poor who is speaking of our social duties, but it is also the bishop who spends many hours of the night in prayer and is ever conscious of the link between God's ascendancy and his own action.

May we, by our joint efforts, help our readers to understand that prayer and the socio-political work of evangelization are intimately united in the life of the Christian who desires to be faithful to the whole gospel, verse by verse.

I will begin by introducing the problem underlying these pages. Then Helder Camara and I will take turns presenting our reaction to each of the aspects that define the complete Christian in his religious, social and apostolic commitment. We will advance our personal opinions, with a proximate unity of vision.

Although I have penned the last chapter, on the political dimension, it translates our common thinking, which, moreover, is the very thought of the Church as expressed in its most official documents, ranging from *Gaudium et Spes*, through Medellin and the 1971 Symposium of Bishops, to the Declarations of the Puebla Conference (Mexico) held in February 1979.

Such is the content of these pages, which we present as the *Malines Document* 3, in the series devoted to the study of the renewal in the Holy Spirit and its human implications in the very heart of the world.

Pentecost 1979   L.J. Cardinal Suenens,
Archbishop of Malines-Brussels.

INTRODUCTION

A Double Approach

The Christian who desires to live and to express his faith in the very heart of the world can, from the outset, choose between two standpoints.

He may begin by fixing his gaze on God and opening himself to the Word of God, to his love and grace, then strive to translate into his daily life the logic of his faith according to all its dimensions and consequences. This path extends from God to mankind.

Conversely, another type of Christian may feel primarily involved in everything that pertains to man and the human community; in these circumstances, he will feel that his priority lies with the world, including its sufferings and its joys. This path stretches from mankind to God.

Two types of Christians are born of this option, depending on whether the emphasis is laid on the spiritual or on the temporal commitment. This diversity gives rise to two major tendencies which, all too frequently, set today's Christians in opposition. It underlies a grievous polarization which must be overcome at all costs.

Divisions and Tensions

The tension between the "spiritual" Christian and the "socially committed" Christian is especially perceptible among the younger generations. The very choice of one of the topics discussed by the Taizé Youth Council, "Social Struggle and Contemplation," indicates how much the

5

problem is central to their preoccupations.

All those who are in contact with the young can attest to their ardent search for balance in this domain. Many young people who opt for social service regard adherence to religion, and to the Church especially, as a kind of alienation, a desertion.

The same tension is to be found in numerous sectors. So many new doubts and misgivings have arisen that the very relevance of evangelization in mission lands is called into question.

Is there any point, people are asking themselves, in continuing to evangelize when the underdevelopment of the indigenous population urgently calls for social, economic and political reforms? Can one proclaim Jesus Christ to whole populations dying of hunger?

In which sense is the gospel the message of salvation and liberation? Is it speaking, primarily, of a religious revelation or of a political revolution?

As we know, an analogous tension is threatening the cohesion of the World Council of Churches. Its members can be roughly divided into those who give precedence to orthodoxy (theological reflection on the doctrinal problems of unity) and those who urge orthopraxy (which aims to incarnate the Christian faith in socio-political deeds). This conflict of tendencies is accentuated by the fact that the churches of the affluent northern hemisphere are confronted with the poor churches of the southern hemisphere, where social oppression is an everyday problem. The WCC Central Committee, convening in Kingston, Jamaica (January 1–12, 1979) has recently held an eventful session in its arduous search for a workable synthesis.

This same tension recurs in the problem of evaluating the spiritual currents now sweeping through the churches—in particular, the renewal in the Spirit, known as the charismatic renewal.

Should it be rejected as a current that might foster alienation, as a factor of social stagnation? — or should it be welcomed as a mighty grace, capable of renewing the springs of
the spiritual life, of revitalizing the Christian existence, and
of uniting Christians in depth?

Is prayer, which this renewal has so vigorously rehabili-
tated, a desertion of responsibility or, on the contrary, an
urge to serve God in the very heart of the world? Is not the
attempt to restore unto mankind the sense of the living God
the supreme social service, which society needs if it is to re-
discover its pivot, its essential balance?

These are so many questions that cannot be evaded — so
many challenges, urging us to work out answers that take
account of the full complexity of reality and of the many
facets of the one gospel.

Mgr. Dondeyne, the eminent scholar of the Philosophical
Institute of Louvain, has pointed out the danger of exclusive
positions as follows:

> To emphasize more clearly that faith is not an alibi and
> that the modern believer must learn to find God in every-
> day life (obviously an excellent thing), some claim that
> preaching and catechesis should centre mainly on the
> second commandment ("Love your neighbour as
> yourself"). "Not everyone who calls me 'Lord, Lord' shall
> enter the kingdom of heaven, but he who does the will of
> my heavenly Father" (Mt 7:21). From this teaching of
> Christ, they deduce that to be a Christian principally
> means to work for the liberation of man and to found a
> more just world.
>
> Of course, they discuss the man-Jesus, and at great
> length, but in order to discern in him the model of broth-
> erly love and the keystone of history. They forget to add
> that he is also the Word of God who, living in the
> Father's bosom, communicates God to us. To believe in

the coming kingdom is to be convinced that, because there is a God, the advent of a more just society is not an idle dream, despite all the failures of the past.

The main task of the Church, as the witnessing people bearing the message, is — according to them — to help the world to come of age. But they seem to forget that the Church's specific mission is also to help the world to find God. As for catechesis, its principal task, they maintain, is to foster in the young that indispensable area of questioning which eventually allows the problem of God to rise to consciousness and the word "God" to become meaningful. But they underestimate the importance of the explicit proclamation of God and of religious education properly so called.[1]

The Necessary Complementarity

The conflict of tendencies, of which I have just indicated a few salient points of emergence, can be understood only in the light of history. All too often, a one-sided position provokes another biased attitude, or a too heavy emphasis produces an excessive reaction in the opposite direction. It is not easy to find the point of equilibrium straightaway. The same is true of the "verticalism/horizontalism" conflict, which nowadays is particularly acute. The so-called "horizontalist" tendency arises, in part, from a legitimate reaction against a "disembodied" Christianity of the "pietist" type, which is not sufficiently mindful of the gospel's social implications. But today we are witnessing the opposite emphasis, which is a reaction against the first and could put at risk the very specific character of Christianity if it were not counterbalanced.

As Etienne Borne has noted, "What is serious is that the debate sets not only Christians against Christians, but also one Christianity against another Christianity."[2]

Here there is a double pitfall to be avoided: that of a disembodied Christianity, and that of a Christianity without the risen and living Christ.

To be a Christian means to be "tuned in" to both Jesus Christ and the world's events; to be open to God in one's very openness to the world; to be at once a man of prayer and a man of action, faithful to Jesus Christ, the only begotten Son of God and the brother of all men.

Each baptized person is, by definition, a member of Christ's Body, called to live in communion with his brothers in faith and, equally, with his brothers in humanity.

The establishment of justice is man's fundamental duty, but this justice concerns both God and one's neighbor.

To be just, we have to respect every right and to give each person his due. God is entitled to our worship and praise: "It is truly right and fitting that we should, at all times and in all places, give thanks to you Lord, holy Father, through your beloved Son, Jesus Christ," we say in the preface to the eucharistic prayer. And did not the Savior himself, to whom we resort as our mediator with the Father, become "our justice," even as he made himself "our wisdom" and "our liberation"?

Justice must be respected and rendered to both God and mankind, inseparably. Poor and rich alike are entitled, in Christian justice, to be nourished by the Word of God. The commandment "Seek first the kingdom of God and his justice" (Mt 6:33) embraces both heaven and earth.

When we peremptorily accuse the "spiritual" Christian of pietism and the "socially committed" Christian of materialism, we are, in fact, doing injustice to both. Verticalism is not an adequate term, nor is horizontalism. The gaze of the crucified Christ is fixed on the Father, and his heart is penentrated with love for all men: the cross is at once vertical and horizontal.

We are pledged, willingly or otherwise, to welcome the

whole of this mystery into our lives: the service of men and the contemplation of God are intimately united. For us, the desertion of the world in the name of God is just as unacceptable as the neglect of God in the name of temporal commitments. The false, disembodied mysticism cannot give way to a political faith that has lost its Christian resonance. What is at stake here is our true identity as men and Christians.

The former Archbishop of Canterbury, Dr Ramsey, having described these two conflicting types of Christian, movingly appealed to them, urging them to understand that these two orientations are not separate but drawn to each other; and he concluded by showing that the witness of the Christian actively involved in the social and political field desperately needs to be completed by the witness of the prayerful and contemplative Christian.

We heartily endorse this poignant appeal. It sums up the whole aim of the following pages.

When engineers carve a tunnel through the mountains (I am thinking, for example, of the St. Gotthard, connecting Switzerland to Italy), they begin the ground work on each of the mountain slopes descending into the valley. The important thing is that the two teams should meet at the precise point that links up the two countries. Likewise, our true meeting point is in Christ; his Spirit prompts our adoration of the Father and guides our service to man. The important thing is to open men to God and to open up for God a path to men. The only difference here is that the initiative comes from God, and it is he who invites all men to collaborate with him.

It is in this spirit that Dom Helder Camara and I have conceived the present document. The chapter sequence clearly translates our unity of inspiration: "Before God," "In the Service of Men," "Apostles of Christ," and "In the Heart of the City."

NOTES

1. A. Dondeyne, R. Guelluy, A. Léonard, *Comments s'articulent amour de Dieu et amour des hommes?*, in *Revue Théologique de Louvain*, 4th year, 1973, fasc. 1.
2. Etienne Borne, *La Croix* (November 13, 1976).

I

BEFORE GOD

Dom Helder Camara

God of All Creation

In varying degrees and with very diverse consequences, the human creature usually discovers the Creator at the heart of his creation. The sky, the sun, and the stars; the sea and the rivers; the mountains and the valleys—all these speak to us in a special way of the Creator and Master.

Usually the human creature feels dwarfed by nature, which is overwhelming in its grandeur and force. The forest, the storm, the wild animals—especially the strongest—prompt man to seek the help and mercy of the Supreme Being, whom he does not see personally, but whose presence and power remain beyond doubt.

When the heavens close and hold back the rain, when animals and plants grow scarce in the regions where they normally find their sustenance, man seeks the protection of the Almighty, who is thought to live beyond the clouds or the highest mountains. And more, man instinctively forms the concept of sacrifice, of killing and immolating living creatures, as if he himself were the victim, offering up his life to gain the good will of the Master of the universe.

Thunder and lightening, he feels, are the manifestations of his Master's wrath. He tries to interpret silence, the winds, the course of the stars.

Almost invariably there are, among the many human groupings, a few men who assume the role of the sacred and present themselves as the privileged interpreters of the Most High, whose will they try to discern.

Below the Supreme Being one finds, in various religions of the world, human groups entreating other, less powerful gods, who are said to control in a special way a few domains or forces of creation. But this is not the vision of Christianity, or of the people of Israel, whose belief in the one God is carried on and deepened by Christianity.

God Reveals His Plan of Salvation

By virtue of a special covenant, willed by God, the Jewish people was chosen, among all the nations, to be a witnessing people, testifying above all to the oneness of God. It recognizes and proclaims one Lord and Master, a very holy God.

God the Creator of the world, in whom we believe, has always wished man to be his "co-creator." He has appointed man to tame nature and to complete his creation.

Not content to know that man, like the whole of creation, is immersed in him, the Lord is everywhere, and it is in him that we breathe and act and find our being. Omnipresent by virtue of his creation, the Lord has established a very special and intimate covenant with man.

He wishes not only to give man being and life, but also to draw him into the very intimacy of his own life. With man he has made a new and definitive covenant.

God of the Incarnation

In ancient days the Lord sent the witnessing people patriarchs and prophets, in order to sustain its faith in the one God. But in the fullness, the zenith of time, he sent his own Son, who took flesh by assuming, in the Virgin Mary, a human nature through the working of the Holy Spirit. God was made man in Jesus Christ.

By coming to us in this way, by living on our earth, Christ brought us a stupendous revelation. He revealed to us that God, the Almighty and the Most High, the Father of all men, wished us to become in Jesus Christ — the only-be-gotten Son — sons by adoption, called to share in the very life of God.

Like his Father who creates with us, God-made-Man, our Brother, wishes us to complete his work of redemption. He desires us to be "co-redemptors," so that liberation from sin and from the consequences of sin may be achieved in us and with us.

Lastly, the Holy Spirit — like the Father sharing his creation with us, and the Son drawing us into his work of redemption — wishes us to collaborate in his permanent work of sanctification. He desires us to be, as it were, instruments of "co-sanctification."

To us human creatures falls the duty of responding to these divine initiatives, which are beyond our boldest dreams.

To the extent that we are conscious of the riches heaped on us, we have to do our utmost — and more — to serve, with all our heart and all our soul, as interpreters of nature and minstrels of God.

The Psalmist teaches us to lend our voices to the whole of creation and, in the wake of St. Francis of Assisi, we are urged to sing the praises of the creatures, including those that come from the Creator thanks to the collaboration of man, his "co-creator."

Without considering ourselves better than anyone else, but by making good use of the riches heaped on us by God, we are called:

— to present our sorrows and needs to the Lord in the

hour of affliction, but equally to open ourselves to the joy of worshipping the Lord, happy in the knowledge that he exists and that he is God;

— to endeavor, permanently, to extend ourselves, to progress beyond selfishness, to enlarge our understanding, our forgiveness, our openness to love;

— to live, very concretely, the Lord's today in the place and the circumstances which he has chosen for us, and to strive, increasingly, to be pilgrims of the Absolute and citizens of the Eternal;

— to look at every human creature, without asking what tongue he speaks or to what race and religion he belongs. The Christian can and must say to himself: "Now *there* is my brother or my sister," and he can and must add: "my blood brother or sister, since the same blood of Christ was shed for both of us, as indeed for all men."

Prayer, the Key to Contact with God

This openness, this responsibility to God, is lived and realized in prayer, which brings us into direct contact with God and puts us through to him. Without prayer, there is no current, no Christian respiration.

Here I venture to bring in my personal experience of the role of prayer in human life. I was ordained priest in my twenty-third year, in 1931. I was then living in Fortaleza, a small capital of North-East Brazil.

From that moment I understood that, in view of my decision to give myself unreservedly to God and my neighbor, it would be absolutely necessary for me to devote space and time to prayer, speaking and listening to God. Otherwise, in no time at all, I would be depleted and have nothing to offer either my brothers or the Lord.

Knowing this to be true, I take advantage of a faculty

that God has given me: that of waking up and falling asleep again at will. Consequently, I wake up every night at two in the morning and remain in prayer for two hours.

Of course, I am not suggesting that I am a great penitent. It is no sacrifice for me to "keep awake and pray." I have discovered that we are doing our soul an enormous injustice if we do not give it the opportunity to refuel itself, in the same way that sleep restores the strength of our body.

There are specific ways of refuelling the mind and the spirit: contact with nature, music, conversation with friends and, for those who are blessed with faith, listening and speaking to the Lord.

So when I wake up at night, my first concern is to restore the unity within me. During the day, it is dispersed: my eyes and arms and legs go in all directions. At those privileged moments of the night, I endeavor to restore the unity of my being, that unity which, from the day of our baptism, is in Christ.

At those moments, a favorite prayer of Cardinal Newman often comes to my lips (here I am quoting it from memory and simply retaining its spirit): "Lord Jesus, do not remain so hidden in me! Look through my eyes, listen through my ears, speak through my lips, act with my hands, walk with my feet... May my poor human presence recall, at least remotely, your divine presence."

For when Christ and I are *one*, how delightful it is to speak to *our* Father in the name of all men, of all times and all places. The two of us having become *one*, we worship our Father (and I cherish in my memory all the most beautiful things my eyes have seen in my life), we give thanks to our Father, we ask his forgiveness (and I like to add: "As for me, Lord, I'm a qualified ambassador of human weakness, because all those sins of men, I too have committed, or could in the future"), and we present the petitions of our brothers.

In my petitionary prayer, I like to tell God of all the things that happened yesterday:

- I met that poor workman, unable to find a job...
  I think of him, concretely. But beyond him, I think (we think) of all the unemployed in today's world.
- Then I encountered that young girl, just awakening to life. I think of her, but beyond her, I think of all the young, with their problems, their hopes, or their distress.

Obviously, I do not forget my breviary (*Prayer for the Present Time*). And, always, the beauty and wealth of those moments come from unity with Christ.

This vigil devoted to prayer prepares me for the eucharistic celebration, the peak moment of the day.

And, by the grace of God, the Eucharist envelops the whole day in wonder, because everything, in all simplicity, becomes Offertory, Consecration, Communion.

I assure you, reader, that in this way the Lord gives me a thousand reasons for living!

Let me also convey to you at least the joy and the beauty of living communal prayer in our grass-roots communities, which we call "basic church communities."

A baptism celebrated by one of our grass-roots communities is quite different from a mere social and family event, which is sometimes reduced to seeking a godfather who will protect the child. With us, the whole church community is involved. The entire community prepares to celebrate the official incorporation of a new member into the Church and the community, which is the living image of Mother Church.

The same is true of the other sacraments. It is not difficult to imagine the power and beauty of a communal confirmation, or again, of a wedding, a priestly ordination, and even an episcopal ordination, celebrated in this spirit.

To hold celebrations of this kind, a price has to be paid: they cannot be improvised or reduced to formalities. But when we behold true community celebrations, we really relive the early days of the Church and come closer to the ideal that eluded us: to be one heart and one soul in Christ.

The Christian, according to his religious dimension, is the well-adjusted follower of Christ: one with Christ and made responsive in him and by him to the whole of human life. He is the Christian who is the universal brother of all men and loves to give prayer its communal dimension, both visibly and within a group.

I have tried to express all this in the simple and humble words of the following prayer:

How poor you will remain
until you discover
that you do not see best
with open eyes.

How naive you will remain
until you learn
that when your lips are closed,
there are silences richer
than torrents of words.

How clumsy you will remain
until you understand
that joined hands can do far more
than restless hands
which may inflict
the unintended wound.

BEFORE GOD

Cardinal Suenens

"To be one with Christ"—this, as Dom Helder has just reminded us, is the aspiration which awakens the Christian's contemplative vocation.

I would like to say, in my turn, what such an aspiration involves today for the person who desires to be a true disciple of the Lord.

Christianity Is Jesus Christ

The religious drama of our time does not primarily reside in the growing scarcity of religious or priestly vocations, nor in the increasing neglect of Sunday worship. Instead it revolves around the lamentable fact that the face of Christ has become blurred in the souls of Christians.

All too often, Christianity is presented to the world as an ideology, a practical wisdom, an option for values. In this light, Christianity is seen as a privileged "ism," but just one of many. Christians urgently need to be reminded that Christianity is Jesus Christ—the one, ineffable Person, whose nature is both human and divine and who is at the heart of the past, present, and future, at the heart of creation and the world.

"Among you stands one whom you do not know": this proclamation of John the Baptist is addressed as much to our contemporaries as to the disciples of the forerunner. Our generation — like the disciples on their way to Emmaus on Easter evening — must encounter Jesus Christ in person, and recognize his presence, his multiple modes of presence, among us.

The sociological situation of Christianity has changed. Christianity is no longer a heritage handed down from father to son; it is no longer integrated into the daily life of our environment. Instead it is rejected or challenged. The Christian existence is no longer taken for granted.

Today, and henceforth, it is even more necessary for the child baptized at birth to take on eventually — and with full awareness — the Christian commitments that were undertaken for him at his baptism. On the threshold of adult life, he will have to discover Jesus pesonally. He will have to relive his baptism "in fire and in the Spirit." With complete lucidity, he will have to let himself be transformed by the Spirit into a living Christian, one who is responsible for his faith and who knows how to translate it into his life, at the very heart of the world.

This new situation requires us to define anew our special features as Christians.

The Specific Traits of Christianity

Today millions of people are seeking a clear answer to the question: what new and specific contribution does Christianity make to an already honorable and generous human life? In which way does a Christian differ from the man who effectively loves his fellow-men? What meaning should we attribute to expressions like those we have just read: "being one in Christ" or "restoring my unity in Christ"? And what did St. Paul mean when he exclaimed: "I live — not I, but Christ in me"? Was this just a lyrical rhapsody, or was it the expression of a lived faith?

As long as the baptized person has not understood and accepted the demands of his baptism, as long as he has not adjusted his life to them, there will be no spiritual renewal in the Church. It is Jesus Christ who defines our specific traits, not us: the norm is not an honest statistic average obtained by observing how the majority of Christians live. To define this norm, we have to answer the precise question: what does the Lord expect of those whom he calls to follow him, and how did the first Christians understand their vocation? The Acts of the Apostles provide the answer.

Normative Christianity

The Acts describe a few traits of the "normal" behavior of the first Christians. "The disciples," we read, "devoted themselves to the apostles' teaching, to the brotherhood, to the breaking of bread, and to the prayers" (Acts 2:42). The image is that of brotherly, eucharistic, spiritual apostolic communities.

Here we see the Christian living a filial relationship with God, expressed through common prayer and especially through the Sunday eucharistic celebration. This Christian also lives in fellowship with his brothers — a fellowship resting on both a harmony of mind and a real concern for the poorest members, a love that extends to the sharing of all goods.

The vertical line of relationship directs him to God the Father, in a surge of adoration, gratitude and entreaty. The horizontal line opens him to other men and their needs. The brotherly sharing that reigns among these Christians strikes observers by its intense charity, "See how they love one another!"

The revitalization of our Christian authenticity also involves these two dimensions.

To measure the gap between the existence of the first

23

Christians and the "normal"—that is to say "normative"—
Christian life, we must, I repeat, ask ourselves the initial
question: What does Jesus expect of his disciples? We tend to
define the Christian in terms of rites, practices, and certain
moral attitudes. But is that the whole of Christianity? Is it
even its principal sign? The gospels and Acts give us quite
another picture: the very name "Christians," given for the
first time to the disciples at Antioch (Acts 11, 26), is
expressive of a fundamental and special relationship with
Jesus Christ, the Risen Lord.

There can be no mistake about the Christian's identity.
The Christian:
- has entered into a personal and living relationship with
  Jesus, whom he acknowledges as his Lord and Savior;
- does not live in isolation, but behaves as a member of
  Christ's Body, because he is integrated into a local
  church community;
- knows that the Master has called him to bear fruit by
  evangelizing and serving his fellow-men.

Such is the original, adult, "normal" Christian. Having
decided to follow the Master, he has agreed to pay the price
of his fidelity, even to the supreme witness, which includes
martyrdom.

"I Live—Not I, but Christ in Me"

We have to recognize that, strictly speaking, there is only
one complete Christian: Jesus Christ himself. But we must
let him transform our lives so that we may thus receive some
of his plenitude.

"I live—not I, but Christ in me." What is St. Paul saying,
if not that the Christian is a man dispossessed of self and
possessed by Christ in every aspect of his daily life?

To live is to see, love, speak, and move. To live in Jesus Christ is to see with his eyes, love with his heart, speak with his lips, and follow in his footsteps.

There is no need here to set out in detail all the religious demands of Christianity. My aim is simply to describe the recognizable, distinctive mark of the Christian who serves his brothers.

The Christian is well-aware of the nobility of service, human solidarity, and philanthropy. But he also feels and knows that he is called to live in communion with the One who loved us to the point of giving up his life for us. This Christian demand obliges us to go out to our brothers with the very love of Jesus Christ. Periodically, the Church reminds us, in the liturgy, of the words of the prophet Ezekiel.

I shall give you a new heart,
and put a new spirit in you;
I shall remove the heart of stone from your bodies
and give you a heart of flesh instead.
I shall put my Spirit in you (Ez 36:25–27).

Loving with the Heart of Christ

God will change your heart of stone and help you to love others with his own heart. A fundamental revolution, a radical transformation. Humanly speaking, we are not capable of loving many people beyond the narrow circle of our family and friends. The human heart is too weak to beat in tune with all the sufferings of men. We easily get tired, and even more so when we have to love, really love, unlikeable people, to say nothing of those who are actively hostile to us. At the very first obstacle our surge of love is halted.

And yet, we are truly living our Christianity, in all its beauty, when we love our brothers not only with our poor hearts, but with the very heart of God. Men do not like to be loved *for* the love of God, that is to say indirectly and in a roundabout way. We have to love them *with* God's very love. It is then that the metamorphosis which transcends narrowness, reticence, and discrimination is achieved.

To echo Cardinal Newman's prayer, of which Dom Helder has just reminded us, I would like to end by quoting these moving lines by Annie Johnson Flint:

> Christ has no hands but our hands
>   To do his work today;
> He has no feet but our feet
>   To lead men in his way;
> He has no tongue but our tongues
>   To tell men how he died;
> He has no help but our help
>   To bring them to his side.
> We are the only Bible
>   The careless world will read;
> We are the sinner's gospel,
>   We are the scoffer's creed;
> We are the Lord's last message
>   Given in deed and word—
> What if the line is crooked?
>   What if the type is blurred?
> What if our hands are busy
>   With other work than his?
> What if our feet are walking
>   Where sin's allurement is?
> What if our tongues are speaking
>   Of things his lips would spurn?
> How can we hope to help him
>   Unless from him we learn?[1]

NOTES

1. *Vocation and Victory — An International Symposium Presented in Honour of Erik Wickberg*, Basel Brunnen Publishinghouse, p.268.

II

AT THE SERVICE OF MAN

Cardinal Suenens

The Christian and His Human Ties

No Christian can live in a vacuum, a private world of his own. Every baptized person must accept responsibility for the social consequences of his Christian way of life. Such a responsibility involves him in a whole network of relationships and duties which ripple outwards, in ever-widening concentric circles, forcing him to opt for or to reject certain values on the family, professional, economic, civic and political planes.

The contemplative life, even in its most radical forms, cannot be an escape from reality; on the contrary, it is an approach to reality that strives to reach down to the depths of the human and Christian existence.

The Christian cannot isolate himself from the world and escape into the wilderness. Each Christian has to participate actively, according to his personal vocation, in the work of humanizing the world, however exacting this task may be.

For the Christian, there can be no question of choosing between contemplative faith and good works, or of setting them in opposition. The Christian has to put his faith to work.

When we stress the importance of social duty, it is wise to remember that everything which fosters better relationships between men, everything that brings into play their brotherhood, is already social action, even if it is not embodied in determined social projects.

If we are to understand what the inspiring social influence of Christians means, both individually and collectively, we have to take a good look at the whole area covered by the term "social," and not restrict social life to just one of its numerous manifestations or expressions. The sociologist Georges Gurvitch has suggested a simple classification which helps to clarify this question. He distinguishes between: (a) *all-embracing societies*, containing social ensembles complete enough to meet all the needs of their members, e.g. a country or a group of countries; (b) *partial groupings*, like the family, kinship groups, voluntary associations, social classes, etc.; and lastly (c) the multiple forms of *social ties*, that is to say, the diverse relations established between the members of a human community.[1]

There are, in fact, countless values of sociability which are both useful and essential to the viability of minority groups, not to speak of larger communities. In all this, "lack of communication" is one of the most serious problems of our time. Practically every branch of knowledge is researching this problem in an attempt to discover how it can be remedied in all human groupings: in marriages, the family, trade, industry, management, and so on. Clearly, the concrete solution to the difficulties affecting each and every human being will have to involve more than just a general change of structures.

All too frequently, the label "social" is reserved for determined projects (reforms) which aim to transform social structures. But the term obviously has a much broader meaning, extending far beyond this restrictive definition.

Speaking of the social impact of the life of faith, hope and charity, Mgr. A. Dondeyne writes:

In this respect, St. Paul's language has a striking and illuminating power. To describe what faith in Christ achieves in the world, Paul speaks of "new creation," of the emergence of "the new self, created in God's way, in true righteousness and holiness"; and again, he speaks of sharing in the life of the risen Christ through the Spirit's action. The fruits of the Spirit, he writes, are "love, joy, peace; patience, kindness, goodness; trustfulness, gentleness and self-control" (Gal. 5:22–23). Clearly, what lived faith achieves is not a flight from the world. But neither does it make the Christian a superman, an exceptional being, exempt from the human condition of the bulk of mankind. What it engenders is an existential quality which transfigures *man's everyday life* [italics added], leading it to more openness, more truth and veracity, more goodness and justice, more freedom and responsibility.[2]

These values of sociability leap to the eye in a really authentic eucharistic celebration, or in a prayer group that is characterized by freedom, mutual trust and a spirit of gratuitousness. There interpersonal relations reach a deeper level of communion, thanks to a common openness to the Spirit of the living God. The fact that each one of the participants is personally called to contribute to the whole assembly's prayer and edification — in the Pauline sense of the term — tends to make it a community of intense participation. This is a highly significant social experience, one which cannot fail to make an impact on other areas of human relations: for instance, on the economic level. The first Christian community offers us a striking example of this social awareness: "The faithful all lived together and owned everything in common; they sold their goods and possessions and shared out the proceeds among themselves according to what each one needed" (Acts, 2:44–45).

In the history of the Church many other examples could be cited of charismatic experiences flowing out to the social and political spheres. And in our own time, figures like Mother Theresa of Calcutta, Martin Luther King, Cesar Chavez and Jean Vanier have shown that private and collective prayer can be a powerful inspiration to action, while cleansing action of all hatred, pride and violence.

The charismatic renewal, which draws its inspiration from the essence of the gospel message, the interrelated charisms of the Spirit, and mutual service, is already, on the strength of all this, contributing to the transformation of social life. But lived faith will also lead men quite naturally to undertake social initiatives as many and as varied as the human sufferings they encounter.

A recent book, entitled *Charismatic Social Action: Reflection — Resource Manual*,[3] proposes a vast range of specific social actions, within the reach of anyone seeking to help the handicapped, prisoners, drug addicts, the aged, the mentally ill, and every kind of underprivileged person. Such assistance extends to vast collective actions for a more just society, human rights, a minimum living wage and a healthier environment.

In this same perspective, we must bear in mind the significant social role played, in the renewal and elsewhere, by small Christian communities who, desiring to serve God and their fellow-men, share a common life and practically all their possessions. They are a living reminder of the primitive communities. Their social service is anchored in the religious life, just as in bygone days our monasteries were places where work and prayer were inseparably united and the rhythm of the liturgy blended with that of the spade and the plough.

Social commitment, I repeat, is not simply an extra moral duty: it is all part and parcel of evangelization. It is in the very name of its gospel awareness that the Church commits itself to everything that makes man more human, to every-thing that liberates him so that he may truly blossom. The 1971 Synod of Bishops emphasized this point in one of its main conclusions:

"Action on behalf of justice and participation in the trans-formation of the world fully appear to us as a constitutive dimension of the preaching of the Gospel, that is to say, of the Church's mission for the redemption of the human race and its liberation from every oppressive situation."

Evangelization and Humanization

Because there is such a close connection between evan-gelization and humanization, it is important not to present the latter as an isolated value necessarily preceding evan-gelization, as suggested by the fallacious slogan: "Let's begin by humanizing the world, and only then can we evan-gelize it." This would mean that we must first rescue man from the evils that alienate him, and then — only then — pro-claim the good news to him. It is a dangerous formula be-cause it implies that the mission of proclaiming Christ to the world must temporarily be shelved until the world has been humanized.

Such a view casts doubt on the very meaning of the Church's apostolic and missionary life, both within and out-side its frontiers. What is questionable in the formula "hu-manize first, then evangelize" is the word "first," that is to say, the order of priorities.

No, we have to carry out the two duties simultaneously. The "first" followed by "then" implies that evangelization is divorced from humanization. This is far from true, for they are interdependent duties.

Men have to be given both the means and reasons for living. Neither of these two duties can cancel the other. As Father Chenu, O.P. has so rightly observed: "Evangelization is of another order than civilization. Feeding men does not automatically save them, even though my own salvation urges me to feed them. Advancing the culture and civilization of men is by no means the same thing as converting them to the faith."

On the other hand, Christ is not only "the soul's life." He wishes to give life to the whole of man. Nothing can elude his ascendancy, for it bears on every aspect of life — family, professional, civic and economic, national and international — and every sphere: leisure, the press, cinema, radio and television, the use of nuclear energy, and so on.

To restrict Christianity to a few pious practices, however important these may be, is to truncate it. It is understandable that on beholding certain atrophied Christian lives, the unbeliever accuses Christians of disregarding or minimizing the human effort, the concern for progress and social justice. However, he should not blame Christianity for this state of affairs but the Christian who betrays his faith by wrongly adducing it to justify his indifference.

We cannot be Christians "only on Sunday," in church. We must live our Christianity right through the day and every week of the year by practising the commandments — and not just the first or the sixth. *All* the commandments and the *entire* gospel must be incorporated into the *whole* of life.

The Sin of Omission

It is also a misconception of true Christianity to reduce it to the negative aspect of the law: "Thou shalt not lie; thou shalt not bear false witness; thou shalt not steal." For apart from evil to be avoided, there lies before us the immense domain of good to be accomplished. A negative good conscience is not enough. For there are such things as culpable omissions and crimes of non-love.

If, in the hour of triumph of the liberal economy, Christians had been keenly aware of their positive social duties on beholding "unmerited destitution" (a phrase of Leo XIII), the social question would not have assumed such dramatic proportions.

And if, in more recent times, nascent Communism had encountered full-blooded Christians, our contemporary history would doubtless have taken another course. Nikolai Berdyaev, the Russian Orthodox philosopher, says as much in these poignant lines written in the thirties: "Bolshevism has been embodied in Russia and triumphed there because I am what I am, because there was no real spiritual power in me, none of the strength of faith that can move mountains; it is my sin and an affliction that is visited on me. The suffering that it has caused me is a satisfaction for my failure and for my iniquity, for our common failure and our common iniquity: all are responsible for all."[4]

Far from inviting its followers to desert the world, Christianity makes it a duty for each baptized person to participate, according to his capacities, in the initiatives of human progress. His respect for his baptism obliges him to fight, to the best of his strength and ability, against poverty and destitution, unemployment and sickness, and social and racial injustice, so that his efforts may hasten the birth of a society that fosters the full development of the human person.

"Other World" and "Other Kind of World"

The Christian's involvement in the temporal and historical is more than a duty prescribed by the world's urgent needs and sufferings. It is an integral part of his relation to God, of the God centered and eschatological aim of his faith and prayer.

As Father Tillard, O.P., writes:

In the Gospel, Jesus links the proclamation of the kingdom with the fulfilment of signs which are, in fact, actions against whatever oppresses man and darkens his existence on this earth. To throw back the curtain of suffering, to knock down the walls of hatred, to bring about a bit more justice and peace on this earth — in short, to work for the "genuine growth of man" in the sense of his dignity — is to serve God objectively, to establish on earth the kingdom whose Lord is Christ today and until he "hands it back to God his Father." Yes, even if in this service the name of the God of Jesus Christ is not uttered.

For this action is carried out *before God*, in communion with his will, which is that our world should become *another kind of world*. He alone judges this action. What the Christian seeks through his action is not primarily the reaction of men, even if they benefit from his endeavour. For his first aim is not to win others by giving them a glimpse of God and the kingdom so that their lives may flow out of the *other world*. It is to obey the Lord's will for this world. Indeed, just as God's will for this *other kind of world* is intrinsically united to his will for the *other world*, the Christian's action for this world aims to open on to a testimony borne to Christ and his Father.

Nevertheless, the immediate and main purpose of his action is collaboration in the transformation of this earth, so that it may be attuned to the *already* of the kingdom which is sown here below. For it is, I repeat, an action carried out *before* God."[5]

In his last public address, in May 1912, William Booth, the Founder of the Salvation Army, gave this moving Christian testimony, at once religious and social; it was his spiritual testament for he died three months later:

While women weep as they do now — I'll fight;
while little children go hungry
   as they do now   — I'll fight;
while men go to prison, in and
   out, in and out, as they do now — I'll fight;
while there is a drunkard left,
while there is a poor lost girl
upon the streets, while there
remains one dark soul without
   the light of God   — I'll fight
                            — I'll fight to
                            the very end![6]

The Holy Spirit and Social Commitment

Scripture and the tradition of the Church both witness that it is the Holy Spirit's action within us which guarantees the authenticity of our relation to God. It is he, the power of fellowship, who ensures the unity of the work of God, the Creator and Father.

Such is the significance of this invocation that the liturgy of the Church places it frequently on our lips: "Send forth your Spirit and they shall be created, and you will renew the face of the earth." Now, these words are far-reaching, and they must be weighed. When we look at the face of the earth, how can we fail to be gripped by fear and even despair? Where are we going? What will happen to the human race if tomorrow some irresponsible person pushes a button that could plunge the world into an apocalyptic nuclear devastation? What will happen when science discovers how to manipulate man at will, even before his birth, and at every stage of his life until his death? How will man behave when political power will arrange for exceptionally effective means of influencing the opinion and action of whole populations?

It is now more essential than ever for Christians to learn what true freedom means, thanks to a renewed openness to the Holy Spirit. They must invoke his active presence in order to cope with problems that imperil our whole civilized way of life. They have to enter the Upper Room, then come out into the public square and bear witness with a humble and brotherly assurance.

The Spirit and His Charisms

The Christian needs the Spirit and his gifts, his charisms, not only for his personal spiritual life, but so that he may contribute to the healing of society's ills. These ills also need to be discerned through the gift of wisdom and subjected to the healing power of the one Savior of the world. The "social" Christian and the "charismatic" Christian both need to surrender, with the same humility, to the action of the Holy Spirit in them, so that through their human and technical collaboration the world may be renewed in depth.

For the sanctifying Spirit and the creative Spirit are one and the same Person. The Spirit respects our human condition; he deepens and strengthens its value. He does not invalidate the play of human factors; on the contrary, he accentuates even the autonomy of our human faculties. And more—he gives them extra strength and makes them effective signs of God's power and goodness.

God means us to be his sons by adoption. The Holy Spirit desires man in his human totality, and he transports man not only beyond his native capacities but beyond his boldest dreams. He calls us and introduces us into the trinitarian mystery, neither more nor less.

As N. Fedorov affirmed in the last century, "Our social programme is the Trinity."[7] We have to enlarge our horizons and the boldness of our faith in the Holy Spirit.

Adrien Demoustier has said:

The Holy Spirit reaches down to that intimate point of our being where our inner life links up with external reality, the spirit with the flesh, speech with silence, the old with the new, death with life, the ordinary with the extraordinary, the charism with the institution, the individual with the collective, and so on.

He constantly orders these two terms to each other in a reciprocity which bestows on the creature's being its likeness to the Creator.

The Spirit acts in man at that point of connection which unifies the complexity of his being."[8]

I believe that we could equally ease the tension between "charismatic" and "social" if we understood the depth and the breadth of the Holy Spirit's action, and if the theology of the charisms progressed beyond and corrected certain too narrow and restrictive exegetic interpretations.

Without the Spirit and his charisms, there is no Church. The charisms belong to the very nature of the Church, understood as the "universal sacrament of salvation" (Vatican II), and they are equally constitutive of the Christian life, as expressed by both the individual and the community.

No group or movement in the Church can therefore claim that the Spirit and his charisms are its private property.

St. Paul enumerates the charisms but makes clear that his list is far from complete. So it is important to understand that the gifts of Spirit cannot be restricted to "extraordinary" manifestations but are manifested in every aspect of the Church's life. The Apostle speaks of them as important experiences in the ecclesial life, but despite their importance, he does not make them the foundation of his theology of the Holy Spirit.

The charisms of the Spirit are beyond number. Thanks to them, each member of the Church is at the service of the whole Body.

Essentially, the charisms are ministerial functions directed to the upbuilding of the Body and the service of the world. In each Christian the Spirit manifests himself by a ministerial function, literally a serving function. No Christian is without a ministry in and for the Church and the world.

The Fruits of the Holy Spirit

The Spirit's action, however interior it may be, is directed to visible fruitfulness in the world around us.

The Spirit bears fruit. Now what does this mean? "The etymological notion of *fruit*," writes M. Ledrus, "corresponds to that of *product* rather than to that of *fruition*, in the sense of enjoyment. In fact, the concept of fruit should be associated with the *fruitful* apostolic union rather than with the fruitious contemplative union... The fruit of the Holy Spirit is a fruit growing out of the spiritual and not just a fruit we relish"[9]

In this light, the "fruit" of the Spirit primarily entails an abundant inner fruitfulness of the God-centered life; but it also implies a repercussion, a creative impact on society, a visible fructification around us in the world. This fructification is like a "divine epiphany in the Christian society." Here, as in every other sphere, the Christian existence, provided it be authentic, visibly overflows with the strength of the inner life and constantly blossoms in the human community.

The World's Suffering in the Light of the Spirit

Every Christian must know that the evils and sufferings of the world cannot be explained solely by human interactions or by the clash of contrary interests. The forces of evil also play a mysterious part in the world's ills, and the power of the Prince of Darkness is not idle. So unless the Christian chooses to live in a fantasy world, he has to be conscious of the wound that original sin has inflicted on humanity. He has to wage his battle for a better world by using the weapons of the Spirit that St. Paul enumerated for the young Church. He has to analyze the evils of society in the light of the Holy Spirit — a light that will lead him to the very source of evil: sin's ascendancy over human weakness.

For we must have the courage to admit that the most serious evil that afflicts us does not reside in institutions or things. It lies in us, in our will, in our soul. This deep interior evil generates ever-recurring social abuses under every regime. And when we fail to attack it at its source, the blame for injustices can be heaped on other people, attributed to other circumstances, but injustice remains.

It can never be too strongly emphasized that sin is intrinsically anti-social. It insidiously weakens ties of brotherhood and threatens the humanization of the world. Our faith tells us, moreover, that it weakens the whole Body of Christ, and that every sin mysteriously strengthens Satan's hold on the world. The world's drama is rooted in a spiritual drama whose stage is quite simply the human conscience. Such a drama always ends up by leaving its mark on concrete facts. Sin, being nihilistic by its very nature, shakes the very foundations of the world, whereas the grace of God regenerates the world and carries it to its highest perfection, both individually and collectively.

Thanks to our faith, we know that no other name but the name of Jesus can, in the last analysis, be the true vehicle of salvation. Without him, we remain on the surface of things. There is a Christian way of working for the general advancement of humanity, and in many social spheres: education, health, the development of the Third World, etc. This in no way excludes the collaboration that the Christian owed to his brothers, his immediate neighbors, especially in a pluralist society like ours. The Christian cannot isolate himself in a ghetto, for he must know that by virtue of his baptism, he is always and everywhere prompted by the Spirit. However difficult may be the problem facing him, he must be ready to believe that the wisdom and power of the Spirit can enlighten and guide him.

The Holy Spirit within us is like a lighthouse projecting its beam on the coast-line and revealing the perils beneath the waves, the hidden reefs. He helps us to discern more clearly everything that is inhuman in the society around us. He obliges us to understand that social conformism conceals abysses of cowardice, of human respect, of fear. He discloses to us today's false gods and denounces our successive idolatries. Today's idols are no longer called Baal or Astarte. They are called the profit-making and consumer society, or again the permissive society, surrendering to the whims of the moment. And we worship them each time we acquiesce to inhuman dictatorships, to unjust wars, to racial discriminations, just "to avoid something worse." In bygone days Christians died because they refused to burn a few grains of incense to an idol. Usually today's Caesar no longer bears a proper name: he is called by the general mood of our time, by the search for "self realization," for personal power, for material prosperity no matter the cost.

We have to keep in our hearts a living hope that carries us towards the glory of God and, *at the same time*, we must work here below with all our strength to make this world of men a happier place to live in. Our vision of the future must increase the value of the present, not depreciate it: every effort that helps men to advance has its own value and is already an anticipation of that "new heaven and new earth," which are being prepared at this moment. At one and the same time, we have to strive towards that "beyond" that exceeds all our dreams and sincerely involve ourselves in God's "today," at the heart of the world.

Because he is the creator of life and the power of fellowship, the Holy Spirit guides us towards concrete, lived experience: the experience of our filial relation to God, and that of our relationship with all men.

It is such concrete experiences, at once grandiose and dramatic, that Dom Helder lays before us in the following pages.

AT THE SERVICE OF MAN

Dom Helder Camara

The Christian, Brother of All Men

The human condition alone already implies a social dimension. No man has been created to live in isolation, in a void. Each one of us is born of a mother and father, who also knew a mother and father. Each one of us lives an incarnation in time and space. And all this creates for us rights and duties with a social dimension.

Whoever believes in God, the common Father of all men, is, on the strength of this alone, committed to ties of human brotherhood and solidarity. In today's world, now that the mass media are acquainting us with our brothers of near and distant lands, we have a clearer perception of the universal solidarity that binds us to them, but also (alas!) of the antagonisms that set nation against nation.

For the Christian—the "new man," as St. Paul calls him—the social dimension corresponds to a new demand made when he encounters other Christian brothers, baptized like him, and members, like him, of one and the same Mystical Body, which is the Church. Of course new duties are emerging, but this brotherhood in Christ does not close the Christian on himself or shelter him in the circle of his Christian brothers: on the contrary, it opens him to the immense world of men for whom Christ shed his redeeming blood and whom the Lord calls, whether they know it or not, to a common destiny.

In his first encyclical *Man's Redeemer*, Pope John Paul II has strongly emphasized how much Christ is present "in the depth of human consciences, reaching down to the interior mystery of man which in the language of the Bible, and even in non-biblical language, is expressed by the word 'heart.'. . . It is He who has restored the divine resemblance, tainted from the time of the first sin. . . Because in Him the human nature was taken up, not absorbed, that nature has, by that very fact, been raised in us as well to an unparalled dignity. For, through his incarnation, the Son of God united Himself, as it were, to every man. He worked with human hands, he acted with a human will, he loved with a human heart. Born of the Virgin Mary, he truly became one of us, in all things similar to us, yet sinless. He is man's Redeemer!" (no. 8).

The Christian who looks at the world with the eyes of faith has a triple duty. According to Cardijn's well-known formula, he has "to see, to judge, and to act."

So let us begin by looking at the world.

Look: The World before Our Eyes

The Christian who looks at today's world is bound to feel severely shaken and challenged by what he sees.

Apparently, the world that extends before our eyes and to which we belong is stronger than ever, more powerful than ever. The advances of science and technology are producing countless surprising creations which our ancestors, if they returned to earth, would consider impossible or interpret as real miracles.

Modern man has technical resources capable of ensuring mankind a human and tranquil standard of living.

Modern man has conquered the great epidemics and the

most serious illnesses. Before long he will, perhaps, dominate death and create life in his laboratories.

Modern man is subduing the rivers, cultivating the deserts, drawing unbelievable riches from the depths of the ocean, and controlling unhoped-for energies, like those of the atom, the sun and the winds. Could it be that he considers the mastery of this tiny earth too insignificant and is setting out to dominate the whole universe?

Yet, for him who has eyes to see, there are obvious signs that this world, apparently so powerful, is in its death-throes.

There are cities growing at such a rate that they are becoming monstrous, cruel, inhuman and, as their population swells, incapable of solving elementary problems like housing, water supply, sanitation, nutrition, and the like. Unemployment is giving rise to theft. Kidnapping and the taking of hostages are making it necessary to establish security measures that are all the more onerous as the ransom demanded and obtained becomes exorbitant. The pollution of our rivers and of the air we breathe is endangering life more and more. The swell of traffic on the roads is an increasingly difficult and nerve-racking problem.

Human creatures have neither the time nor the peace of mind to do credit to their humanity. Many have become robots, numbers. Privacy is beginning to disappear. With such changes—brutal and violent changes of values, for which very few are prepared—recourse to psychiatrists and psychoanalysts has become almost obligatory.

An even more alarming sign that the world is in its death-throes is that over two-thirds of the world's population are living in subhuman conditions, while some superpowers have fifteen or twenty times more resources than are needed to destroy life on earth. And, as if the nuclear and bio-chemical arms race were not enough, these superpowers are coming perilously close to meteorological warfare.

Judging as a Christian

But the Christian's duty is to judge as well as to look. He cannot allow himself to be taken in by this giant with feet of clay.

The world, as he sees it, before his eyes, obliges the Christian to examine his conscience. What have we done with Christ's message of universal brotherhood? How dare we look at Christ if we who wear his name as our shield and call ourselves his disciples are contributing, for our part, to the scandal of this century: a small minority enjoying vast means of existence and enrichment while the great majority of God's sons are reduced to a subhuman existence?

What must we really try to do at the levels of the person, the community, and our peoples? Dare we look squarely at this immense disorder and social imbalance?

Should not our very first step be to seek the causes, to see clearly what is happening with the unjust structures that are crushing over two-thirds of the human race?

Why do we speak of structures? Are they forces that work together and, thus combined, intensify each other? And what are those forces? Who directs them? Who has power of decision over them? Are some of the pressures made on them valid pressures?

How should these unjust structures be judged in the light of the gospel? Are they really unjust? At the root of those injustices, is there, as some maintain, the temptation to "productivism," which was, is and will remain the desire for profit? Let us go further and ask if it is true that egoism is responsible for this insatiable greed for profit.

Is it true that there is an individual egoism? —that there are familial, communal and national egoisms? These questions cannot be evaded.

Acting: With Not For

But it is not enough to see clearly and to judge in the light of the gospel: It is absolutely essential to *act*.

The Christian cannot read the Bible and hear what God says through the prophets, who denounced the injustices of their time, without concluding that the prophetic word is still valid for us and for our time.

He has to look for workable solutions, explore various tracks, learn through trial and error, and evaluate the results so that he may improve them or, on the other hand, extend and develop them.

The key principle for righting the situation in the so-called underdeveloped countries is based on the fact that it is not enough to work *for* the people; one has to work *with* them, to awaken their initiative, to help them be self-sufficient. "Help me to manage without your help" is the cry of every child who wants to grow; it is the general law of education in the widest sense of the word.

By virtue of this principle, laymen, nuns and priests are dedicating themselves to subhuman regions where destitution and hunger reign. Even when they wear no visible religious badge, they are recognized by the light of Christ radiating in them.

The temptation of a people endured to long centuries of domination, which have deprived them, and still deprive them, of the right to think, to make decisions and to act, is to wait passively until they are told what they must do. When the lay and religious animators who devote themselves to them tell these poor people that they have not come to think or to act *for* them but *with* them, they come up against the fear of brutal repression; the poor do not dare to speak, to express themselves, to act, for fear of being crushed by the strong.

*A Hopeful Sign: Grass-Roots Communities

A particularly effective way of helping the poor to right the situation is to encourage them to set up *grass-roots communities*. For in these we find a community spirit that lives on the gospel and draws its strength from Christ. It is important that these communities should spring up and get together in unity, not in order to trample on the rights of others, but to prevent others from trampling on their rights.

Experience shows that it is easy for the powerful to crush one, five or even ten people. But no human force can crush a coherent community, for it is a living God who dwells there and listens to the outcry of his people.

To wait for the human advancement of the people to be achieved from outside, with the help of the powerful, is to expose the people to ever-recurring disillusionment.

But now a song of freedom is really beginning to rise from the oppressed masses of the Third World. All over, the humble ones, the exploited, are uniting with other humble and exploited ones.

The grass-roots communities of the so-called "underdeveloped" countries have a faith, hope, and love nourished by a living liturgy: they live the Eucharist and the sacraments as a community and consequently the liturgy plays an irreplaceable role in their lives. In these communities all the members — children, adolescents and adults alike — shoulder their responsibilities. They participate in the political life, the activities of the trade unions, the cultural life. They are constantly open to all the expressions of a genuinely democratic life.

But listen carefully, for I emphasize this point! Anyone who wishes to animate the grass-roots communities of the underdeveloped countries must have the gift of working not only for the people, but with the people. The people have a sixth sense by which they discern who possesses or does not possess this particular charism of working with them.

Let me speak plainly: the very least one is entitled to expect from all Christians and all men of good will is that they should be impelled by a love of justice to champion the cause of the grass-roots groups in these suffering countries and to defend them against the insidious accusations of those who, out of self-interest, want to avoid the liberating moral pressures of these remarkable groups, which are surely stirred by the Lord's Spirit.

Let us look more closely at the changes of attitude that are incumbent on us and try to discern what we, as a Church, have the duty to awaken, welcome and inspire.

Our Responsibilities

Quite a few people are of the opinion that, in the fight against the unjust structures which are increasingly oppressing countless children of God, the essential, the most difficult and urgent duty is to change the internal structures.

It is obvious that we cannot neglect the aspect of personal conversion and, in this connection, we are deeply indebted to the charismatic movements which invoke the Spirit of God, immerse themselves in prayer, and endeavor to stir consciences.

We must never forget that egoism and its consequences subsist in man. There is personal sin and collective sin. There is the mystery of iniquity. There is not only the world that men know to be the Father's creation, but also the "world" that is synonymous with sin.

Religious Educators

Father Arrupe, General of the Society of Jesus, has stirred the Catholic conscience by emphasizing in a message the urgent need for a profound change in the orientation of our educational work.[10] It is essential that our efforts as educators should aim to form human beings who care for their fellow-men, for justice and social action.

May each priest be fully aware that his mission is to awaken consciences. Let him preach sermons with this aim, especially on Sundays and feast days. Let us imagine for a moment that we no longer had to listen to hollow, vague, bodiless sermons which never question us, or challenge us, or disturb our selfish complacency. I am not asking for sermons that wound for the sole pleasure of wounding, sermons that affront and offend. The more the truth proclaimed is serious, the more it is important to feel that the preacher is speaking as a friend, a brother. If he wounds, he does so in order to heal, like the surgeon. If he scorches, he does so to destroy error, to conquer evil, and far more importantly, to cleanse and purify.

What a responsibility that is, especially for those who preach spiritual exercises, or animate houses of prayer and deep encounters with God! The Spirit of God cannot and must not be invoked in order to nurture alienations. Does not scripture tells us that he who claims to love God whom he does not see, yet hates his brother whom he sees, is a liar? What can we do to magnify the glory of God? We can, and indeed we must, work with all our heart so that the children of God, redeemed by the blood of Christ, may never again divide themselves into oppressed and oppressors.

Nuns and Teachers

In the sphere of education there are so many nursery schools, kindergartens, primary schools, high schools and universities run by Christians! How wonderful it would be if all this immense effort were effectively channelled into the work of overcoming egoism and the unjust structures which are crushing millions upon millions of human beings, our own brothers!

The Mass Media

And what about the all-powerful mass media? It cannot be denied that they are nearly always controlled by powerful interests. We who have the grace and the responsibility to measure the importance and urgency of helping to overcome human egoism and of educating people to care for their neighbors, must seize every opportunity to transmit this message through the press, radio, cinema, and television.

We undergo the influence of the mass media passively, like a sandy beach absorbing the waves of the sea. We have to awaken consciences and stimulate them to react. In countries where freedom exists, it is essential to educate public opinion to the duty of speaking out, of protesting, of launching campaigns for the improvement of physical and moral health.

Here we have an enormous field, left fallow by worthy people, by the resigned silent majority. There is an education in non-violence which opens up unexplored possibilities of righting wrongs, of changing what has to be changed.

Let us always remember that all this must be achieved with no ambition to dominate or to gain prestige but simply to serve the common good. There are valuable latent forces which have to be channelled into liberating moral pressures, capable of ensuring justice and love, which pave the way for true and lasting peace. But it is essential for all men of good will to combine and coordinate their efforts.

Convergence of Efforts

Let us take an example which can easily be multiplied: that of the Church in Latin America.

The Latin American continent has about 170,000 religious (140,000 nuns and 30,000 male religious), scattered throughout the countries of Central and South America.

Latin American also has 800 bishops, members of CELAM (Council of the Latin American Episcopate). Our Church thus reaches 800 dioceses which, in their turn, mobilize the parishes, the grass-roots communities, the priests, and especially the laymen, ever-increasing in number and in devotion.

At the continental level the 170,000 religious are members of CLAR (the Latin American Conference of Religious). Clearly, a great influence can spring from such a convergence: no one can fail to realize that the nun and the religious are servants who have consecrated themselves to God and, consequently, to their neighbor.

If, as solitary and isolated individuals, the bishop, the priest, the religious, or the nun denounce even the obvious and glaring injustices, and if, also on their own, they work for the human advancement of the oppressed, they will most probably be accused of meddling in politics, of rousing the masses, of preaching Communism. If, on the other hand, all our people united, attesting that they were working along the lines of the gospel, of Vatican II, of Medellin and, today, of Puebla, they would be invincible, and we could thus shake the foundations of the oppressive structures.

An Appeal to Christian Courage

The righting of unjust situations is a challenge to all of us. True mystery and wonderful miracle — God has awakened in all the countries, races, religions, and human groupings, people who are resolved to work for justice as the road to peace.

In this work, the Church, in collaboration with all men of good will, has a specific role to play. But it can do this only at the price of a few sacrifices.

If the Church is to give the example it must, if it is to be the living presence of Christ among men and with men, it urgently and permanently needs to cast off its concern for prestige, to unharness itself from the chariot of the mighty, and to agree to live the prophecy of the Master, which is valid for all times: "Behold, I send you out as sheep in the midst of wolves... They will hand you over to courts of judgment" (Mt 10:16–17).

Why should we be afraid to see our peaceful battle for justice wrongly interpreted, wrongly judged, when Christ himself was called an agitator, a subversive element, an enemy of Caesar? If it is true that he was sacrificed because he proclaimed himself Son of God, it is also true that on top of his cross it was written in three different languages that he had been put to death for a political reason, for having declared himself King.

This is the difficult and radiant poverty that God asks of his Son's Church today: to sever all compromises with governments and the powerful, and to commit itself to the service of the poor, the oppressed, the destitute, the sons of God who are made to live subhuman lives.

If we allow ourselves to be conquered by fear or by the prudence of the flesh, to the detriment of the prudence of the Spirit, we will see a growing number of our most active Christians — and especially the young, disillusioned by the faint-heartedness of the Church — leaving us and making their way towards radicalization and violence. Many of them accept Christ and, with him, the prophetic Church, but not the hierarchic and institutional Church. They must be able to see the coherence between theory and practice, that is to say, our firm resolve to live our doctrine.

The day the Church loses the fear of being accused of meddling in politics (because it proclaims the exigencies of the common good), the day the Church does all it can — and more—to bring to life its great texts, its great encyclicals, and the teaching of Vatican II, many of those who consider themselves to be Christians but have distanced themselves from religious practice will be there, body and soul, to help the Church bring its contribution to the creation of a more just and more human world.

Then, and only then, will union and even perfect unity be established between the prophetic Church and the institutional Church, two aspects of the one Church of Jesus Christ.

If we live all this, no Christian or group of Christians will feel the need to go elsewhere in search of other prophets: Christ yesterday, today, and tomorrow will be a sufficient guide and inspiration for them.

In Brief

At the end of this rapid survey of our everyday realities, I would like to summarize my deepest social convictions, which have ripened over the years:

- I do not desire a hostile confrontation between the rich world and the poor world.
- I believe in the violence of the peacemakers, in the moral pressure that liberates man.
- I cannot believe that the universe, created through love, will end in hatred.
- I would like to say to everyone:
  - Where man is, the Church must be present.
  - The egoism of the rich presents a more serious problem than Communism.
  - Today's world is threatened by the atom bomb of squalid poverty.
  - Profound changes must be made in order to establish justice in every sphere, throughout the world.
  - Without a deep personal conversion, no one can be-

come an instrument for the conversion of the world.

— The social revolution will not be achieved in the developing countries unless there is a parallel moral and social revolution in the developed countries.

— We have to build on solid ground. It is not enough to conduct literacy campaigns for the masses. The work, the real work, consists in awakening consciences so that the masses may eventually become a people.

— To revolutionize the world, the only thing needed is for us to live and to spread the gospel of Jesus Christ with real conviction.

— Dire poverty is revolting and degrading; it taints the image of God in every man.

— We have no right to blame God for injustice and its attendant evils; it is for us to do away with injustice.

— My door and my heart are open to all — to all without exception.

— Christ has prophesied what will happen at the last judgment: we shall be judged according to the way we have treated him in the persons of the poor, the oppressed, the downtrodden.

The Voice of the Voiceless World

Let me now turn to God and translate in my prayer the hope of those who are voiceless in a world that crushes them:

Father
how can we fail
to gather all mankind
into prayer,
since your Divine Son,
our brother,

Jesus Christ,
shed his blood
for all men,
of all lands,
of all times?

But hear, O Lord,
my special prayer
for my people,
the voiceless ones.
There are thousands
and thousands
of human creatures
in the poor countries,
and in the slums
of the rich countries,
with no right
to raise their voices,
no possibility
of claiming
of protesting,
however just
are the rights
they have to uphold.

The homeless,
the starving,
the ragged,
the wasted,
with no chance
of education,
no work,
no future,
no hope;
they may end up

believing
it was meant to be,
and losing heart,
become the silent,
the voiceless ones.

If all of us
who believe in You
had helped our rich brothers,
by opening their eyes,
stirring their consciences,
the unjust
would not have advanced,
and the gap
between rich and poor,
between individuals and groups,
between countries,
even between continents,
would not be so glaring.

Do in us, O Lord,
what we have failed
and still fail
to do.
How difficult it is
to get beyond the barrier
of Aid, of gifts,
of assistance,
and reach the realm
of justice!
The privileged grow angry:
our judgment
is unfair, they say.
Meanwhile they discover
subversion

and Communism
in the most democratic,
the most human,
the most Christian Gestures!
Amen.

Puebla Replies

The third Latin American Episcopal conference, officially convoked and opened by the Holy Father, John Paul II, solemnly declared:

This Latin American Episcopal Conference declares itself committed to the poor and condemns as being contrary to the Gospel the extreme poverty that reigns on our continent.

It is striving to gain knowledge of and to denounce the mechanisms which engender this poverty.

It is uniting its efforts with those of other Churches and with all men of good will in order to uproot this poverty and to create a more just and more fraternal world.[11]

NOTES

1. G. Gurvitch, *Twentieth Century Sociology*, New York, 1945.
2. In *Revue Théologique de Louvain*, 1973, p. 9.
3. Sheila Macmanus Fahey, *Charismatic Social Action*, New York, Paulist Press, 1977.
4. N. Berdyaev, *The End of Our Time*, London, Sheed and Ward, 1933, p. 134.
5. "Vie consacrée 'active' et insertion dans le monde du travail,"

in *Vie consacrée*, 15 September 1977, No. 5. A recent work by the same author is significantly entitled *Devant Dieu et pour le monde*, Paris, Cerf, 1974.

6. *Cf. Bernard Watson, A Hundred Years' War: the Salvation Army 1865-1965*, London, Hodder and Stoughton, 1964, p. 15.

7. Cited by Olivier Clement, *Le Monde*, 16-17 July 1978.

8. Adrien Demoustier, S.J., in the review *Christus*, No. 93, p. 114.

9. Art.: "Fruits du Saint-Esprit," in *La Vie Spirituelle*, 1947, p. 717.

10. Letter of Father Arrupe to the religious of the Society of Jesus.

11. *The Present and Future of Evangelization in Latin America* (Conclusions of the Puebla Conference, Nos. 924 to 926).

III

APOSTLES OF CHRIST

Cardinal Suenens

Send Forth Thy Spirit and They Shall Be Created

The term "apostolate" covers a wide range of realities. Here it is understood in its primary religious sense as the direct apostolate which aims to make Jesus Christ and his gospel known to all mankind and to translate them into life. In this sense, it is the response to the Master's order: "Go out to the whole world; proclaim the Good News to all creation" (Mk 16:15). And it flows from Jesus' promise to his disciples: "You will receive power when the Holy Spirit comes on you, and then you will be my witnesses in Jerusalem and in all Judea and Samaria, and to the ends of the earth" (Acts 1:8).

The apostolate that we will discuss in this chapter is directly linked with the mystery of Pentecost, when, through the mouth of Peter, the apostles first proclaimed the wonders of God.

Pentecost evokes tongues of fire over the heads of the apostles: the symbol of the mission of Christians throughout the ages, the answer to Jesus' prayer: "I have come to bring fire to the earth, and how I wish it were blazing already!" (Lk 12, 49).

To receive the Spirit and to witness to Jesus are one and the same thing: it is only to reveal him that the Spirit comes.

It has been rightly said that "The Renewal in the Spirit was not granted to us so that we might become a club of Charismatics; it was given for the evangelization of the world"[1] — in other words, to hasten the coming of God's Kingdom among us. And this concerns all mankind.

The Christian apostolate directly continues the mission of Jesus. Christ will always be born invisibly in human souls, under the action of the Holy Spirit. But Jesus came among us to assume the human condition and to live right in the midst of men. Evangelization prolongs both the mystery of Pentecost and the mystery of the Incarnation. In the first part of this chapter, I would like to underline the first aspect: the pentecostal apostolate, and then to stress, in the second part, the various ways in which the apostolate is incarnated in today's world.

Apostolate through the Word

Faith is proclaimed; it is "good news," eagerly communicated: "I believed, and therefore I spoke," says St. Paul (2 Cor 4:13). Here we have a logical connection. In normal circumstances, faith and non-communication are mutually exclusive.

Confession of faith is inherent in Christianity. A Church which was not a "confessing" assembly, but merely a "ritual" or a "silent" one, would by no means respond to the mission it has received: to witness to Jesus Christ and to give him to the world.

"For whoever would save his life will lose it," said Our Lord (Mk 8:35). The same is true of faith: it remains alive as long as it is contagious and gives itself to others. A faith choked with ashes is bound to die away: like fire, it needs to set ablaze whatever it touches.

The Spirit is given to the apostles of Christ precisely so that they may witness to their faith through the power of the word: The pentecostal tongues of fire are the symbol of this power, and the charisms of the Spirit are largely given with a view of this mission.

We are all familiar with St. Paul's various enumerations of the charisms, particularly those found in Rom 12:6–8; 1 Cor 12:8–10 and 28–30; and Eph 4:11. It is, of course, possible to deepen the exegesis of these charisms, to adumbrate various classifications and to elaborate learned typologies. One may seek to extend their application, to modernize it, or to renew their human armature. But, clearly, there is a series of gifts needing no intellectual sleight of hand, because they aim to present the message directly and, consequently, to give it its full legitimacy in the Spirit.

Thus, 1 Cor 12:8 alludes to the utterance of wisdom, to a message resting on knowledge; Rom 12:7–8 evokes teaching and exhortation; 1 Cor 12:9–10 also lists the gift of faith and that of interpretation, not to mention prophecy which, in one form or another, is regularly cited. In enumerating all these charisms, St. Paul obviously has in mind the apostolate of the word.

"The World Is Simply Not Ready to Listen"

Today a whole trend of thought is attempting to reduce the Christian to silence and adducing countless "reasons" in support of a mute Christianity. The first of these allegations is that our contemporaries *are not ready to hear us.*

To this claim there are two compelling answers. The first: "Do you suppose that the contemporaries of Jesus were ready to listen to him?" We need only look at a crucifix to find the reply to that one. And what about the time of the Apostles? Just think of Paul addressing the Areopagus in Athens and of the reaction of the public: "We'll hear you on this subject some other time" (Acts 17:32).

And the second answer consists of a question: "Is it *true*

that the world isn't ready to hear the Christian message?" For my part, I believe that every man who is seeking the *why* of life, of suffering, of death, betrays a deep longing, and that this silent cry is more poignant than ever in a world bogged down by the contradiction between the dizzying progress of his means of existence and the terrifying withdrawal of his reasons for living.

"The Human Conscience Must Be Respected"

Another way of inhibiting the apostolic élan is to maintain that one must avoid every form of apostolate in order to respect each person's freedom of conscience.

It is undoubtedly true that the human conscience must be respected. We have to admit that in the past our faith was not always communicated with respect for the freedoms of the individual. Conversions "in the Charlemagne style" or as a result of applying the Treaty of Westphalia (*cujus regio, illius et religio*) are deplorable historical facts which cannot be denied. Happily, we have left those times far behind. But it requires quite a stretch of the imagination to claim that one is equally violating consciences by expressing one's faith with warmth and conviction. There is, of course, an unsound, propaganda-motivated kind of proselytism which must be permanently dismissed.

It is normal and indeed required that I should confess my faith by testifying to my Christian experience and to my profound belief which is the mainspring of an immense happiness. But I must always do this with infinite respect for the freedom of others.

We need to renew our understanding of the Master's evertopical words: "I have come that they may have life, and have it more abundantly" (Jn 10:10). In Christ the Christian possesses an increase of life which he cannot keep for himself alone. Of course the grace of God is such that it goes far beyond visible mediations, but what a blessing it is for men to know explicitly the God of Our Lord Jesus Christ, the mystery of his trinitarian life, and the breadth of a love which extends from the Creation to the Parousia by way of the mysteries of salvation!

What an enrichment it is to belong to the living communion of the mystics and the saints who have succeeded one another through the ages and are the glory of the living Church, the pledge of its fidelity before God! The elder brother of the parable, who stays at home, does not appreciate all that he owes to his father and his family, for he takes their love for granted; but the prodigal son — precisely because he has strayed far from home — comes to appreciate these blessings much more deeply than his brother.

This message must also get through to those undisturbed Christians who complacently take their blessing for granted; they must not be insensible to the world's spiritual distress. If they have any doubts about the prevailing religious famine, they have only to look around them, and they will see sects teeming everywhere because we have failed in our task as witnesses.

The Lord has asked us to love God with all our heart, all our soul, all our strength. There is a strength in man, the creative imagination, which deserves special mention. We have to take the duty of "going forth to spread the gospel" very seriously, using all the paths available to us. These paths range from door-to-door conversations to world-wide television transmissions, as well as the endless variety of social communications media at our disposal. Our Lord asks us to shout the good news from the roof-tops: he asks his disciples to be at least as resourceful as the shrewd men of the world. The wealth we have to hand on to others is a word of life which men need more than bread. We have to go out to them and bring them this food.

Apostolate through Life

The reticence displayed by many Christians today when it comes to uttering an explicit and direct word of life, does, however, have one element worthy of attention. Our contemporaries are saturated with ideological discourses and advertising jargon. That is why the Christian apostolate cannot stop short at the verbal message; it has to be incarnated and visible in the very life of the witness. It is principally through what we *are* that we teach others: It is life which illuminates the words we utter and gives them their penetrative power. St. John says of Jesus that "his life was the light of men" (Jn 1:4). The same is true for each witness to Jesus.

More than ever, the world needs Christians made luminous and transparent by the light of Jesus Christ. Paul VI said that the world needed witnesses more than masters. We need less words and more examples. The world needs to discover Christianity in the everyday life of Christians. Like children, it needs a catechism illustrated by brilliantly projected pictures.

The Christian must proclaim the gospel by his whole way of life. And he can do this in two ways that are intimately united: through his positive testimony to the coherence of his faith, his life, options, preferences, and refusals; and also through repentence—the humble and brotherly avowal, before God and men, of everything which, in his private and social life, is a denial of Love. To recognize that one does not love, or does not love enough, is also to bear witness to Love.

As long as the Christian is "humanly explicable," he astonishes no one; he does not challenge the rules of the game or the prevailing conformism. But from the moment that he lives his faith, he presents a problem. He disturbs complacent minds by the questions he raises around him.

Through his whole existence and in all its aspects — marriage, family, profession, civic and social responsibilities — the Christian must illustrate the vital principles that guide him.

Now, what is it in a man that "speaks" to others? Words, obviously, but also gestures, actions, an approach, a quality of life. Revelation itself, as the theology manuals have always reminded us, unfolds through speech but also through deeds — a distinction well brought out by the German terms *Wortoffenbarung* and *Tatoffenbarung*. Vatican Council II declares that divine revelation culminates in Jesus Christ because he fulfills it "*through his whole presence* and by manifesting himself through his words and deeds" (*Dei Verbum*, no. 4).

"Through his whole presence." The person who transmits a message through concrete facts, through his achievements and his whole way of life, opens up a perspective that embraces far more than the one evoked by "doctrine" alone. To affirm this in no way depreciates doctrine, but sets it as a central value in a wider and more encompassing context: the person.

Georges Gusdorf has analyzed as a philosopher the creative power of speech, the human reality which gives meaning to the world. He describes with great insight the incomparable brilliance of the "spoken," the formulated, but urges us to progress further. He points out that the master's teaching counts less than "the witness of his attitude, the incantation of a gesture and a smile." Similarly, he goes on to say, "the presence of Jesus signified for each of his followers a direct and living relationship, within which the word became vocation, an encounter of being with being, and the few words actually pronounced give us but a vague, approximate idea of what really happened.[2]

In his Apostolic Exhortation *Evangelii Nuntiandi*, Paul

VI wrote: "It is primarily by her conduct and by her life that the Church will evangelize the world, in other words, by her living witness of fidelity to the Lord Jesus — the witness of poverty and detachment, of freedom in the face of the powers of this world, in short the witness of sanctity" (no. 41).

So at one and the same time we have to make the good news audible through the witness of a "confessing" faith and visible through life witness. Verbal witness by itself risks remaining abstract and always inadequate in its human expression. Alone and unaided, it addresses itself to the intellect, offering it a truth to be welcomed. Life witness more directly reaches the whole of man and responds to his fundamental aspirations. But these two forms of witness support each other, as St. Paul already emphasized in his Letter to the Thessalonians: "When we brought you the Good News, it came to you not only as words, but in the power of the Holy Spirit and as utter conviction" (1 Thes 1:5).

Apostolate through the Communal Life

It has been rightly said that what the Church needs today, more than new institutions or programs, are vital Christian communities.

As we know, it is precisely in this way that Christianity developed: it grew out of Christian communities, described in the Acts of the Apostles as follows: "The faithful all lived together and owned everything in common; they sold their goods and possessions and shared out the proceeds among themselves according to what each one needed. They went as a body to the Temple every day, but met in their houses for the breaking of bread; they shared their food gladly and generously; they praised God and were looked up to by everyone. Day by day the Lord added to their community those destined to be saved" (Acts 2:44–47).

It was essential for the Christians of the nascent Church to counter the pagan environment of their time with a supportive community life.

Today, in our "postconciliar" world, the same necessity is reasserting itself. The "communal" life entails, in varying degrees, the sharing of life and possessions. The power of Christian survival and apostolic penetration that resides in such a fellowship is undeniable.

The future of the Church will largely depend on the witness of these Christian communities, which are springing up practically everywhere as centers of hope.

Helder Camara has stressed the importance of the grassroots communities on his continent, and the declarations of Puebla strikingly confirm their importance. In my book *A New Pentecost?*, a chapter entitled "The Holy Spirit and New Communities" is devoted to this very question. The steadily increasing dechristianization of the world confirms the soundness of Steve Clark's diagnosis, which I have quoted in that chapter:

A Christian must have an environment in his life in which Chistianity is openly accepted, talked about, and lived if he is going to be able to live a very vital Christian life. If he does not have this, his whole life as a Christian will be weak and might even die away. Yet fewer and fewer Catholics are finding such an environment... When society as a whole cannot be expected to accept Christianity, then it is necessary to form communities within society to make Christian life possible... Because they had been taught to identify "what was right" in matters of religion with "what was accepted by society as a whole," most people began to weaken in their Christian conviction and their Christian living when they saw that Christianity was not being accepted by society as a whole the way it had been.[3]

71

Questions for Today's Apostolate

Having recalled the way of life inspired by the Spirit at the beginning of the apostolic age, and having considered the experience of the primitive community, let us now turn to the Church of our time, where one misunderstanding or another occasionally arises between those who are working for economic and social liberation and those who believe themselves called to a direct and religious apostolate. The latter are asking themselves a few questions and submitting them to the reflection of their fellow Christians.

All the political and social alienations have not yet been removed — far from it! But should one be wholly occupied with those situations and thus be responsible for another frustration and alienation — this time of the religious kind — by neglecting the explicit proclamation of the religious message: the mercy of God, the coming of the Lord, the paschal mystery, eternal life? For it is a fact that every country and every region cannot be considered naturally Christian, deeply rooted in their faith: one need look no further than Europe to see how true this is.

Latin America has come to know by bitter experience, repeated day after day, the violence inherent in authoritarian and implacable systems. Besides, every month brings us a new book relating the disillusionment of Socialists who have discovered the serious blemishes of regimes claiming that they are guided by the same Socialist ideology. The truth is that, regardless of the political regime, or the cultural system, or the overall economic structure, man remains a frail, weak and imperfect being, and so he will always remain to an appreciable degree. Very many revolutionaries become dogmatic, capricious and brutal. In every human society there are people who steal, lie, cheat, betray and murder. But might we not say that this very inhumanity calls to what is human in man, as a personal moral exhortation, directly challenging him as a believer to communicate his spiritual life to others? And will there not always be a very obvious need for this form of apostolate?

Then we must ask, are there not evils from which it will never be possible to deliver man? For instance, his sometimes considerable limitations, both physical and mental; the illnesses and the wretchedness inherent in every human existence, even that of the privileged individual; the pain and the torments born of a misunderstood, rejected, shattered love; the unavoidable wrenches of departure and death — and so many other sufferings? Are not those who suffer bodily and mentally in these many ways — whether or not they hope for a political and economic liberation — entitled to hear the words that the Lord addressed to all those who were heavily tried? Are not those the ones for whose sake he came to dwell among us?

We are called to celebrate mankind's liberation religiously, but there are various levels of liberation. Economic and political liberation has to be celebrated, because it is a "salvific process and the growth of the kingdom," at least "insofar as liberation means a greater fulfillment of man."[4] But there are other levels of liberation, and notably the deeper level where "Christ makes man truly free, that is to say, enables man to live in communion with him; and this is the basis for all human brotherhood."[5] This is a liberation of the religious and spiritual order, and it has a central place in the mystery of salvation. Very many people are more or less consciously awaiting that liberation. Is it not our duty to answer their cry? And did not Our Lord say: "This you ought to have practiced, without neglecting the other" (Lk 11:24)? These words hold true for all time.

APOSTLES OF CHRIST

Dom Helder Camara

And Thou Shalt Renew the Face of the Earth

Charismatics, my brothers! Today God is using the charismatic movement to remind us all of the Holy Spirit's permanent and beneficent action.

Far too many Christians used to think of him as a vague, distant reality, a name one pronounced on making the sign of the cross, a person who had played a particular role on the day of Pentecost and during the early days of Christ's Church.

Those who opened the Bible would find a veiled mention of his presence when they read that at the beginning of the world the Spirit hovered over the waters and made them fertile. They also knew that he spoke through the Old Testament prophets.

The Christian had heard his name on receiving the sacrament of Confirmation. But the invocation of the Holy Spirit was generally confined to the memory of his past interventions; we did not give him his full place in the here and now of our Christian life.

The charismatic movement is helping us to be aware of the wonderful realities linked with the Spirit of God — realities which we ourselves, Christians though we are, had practically forgotten.

Many will remember that during Vatican Council II a celebrated discussion brought about a confrontation between those who wished to relegate the charisms of the Holy Spirit to the past, as if his gifts had only been provisional aids to the Church's expansion in the early years, and those who wished to underline their permanent actuality, which the Council did, in fact, confirm.

Charismatics, my brothers! You who are given the grace to believe that as a Church we are living an unceasing Pentecost, can and must help our present-day Church of Christ tremendously, and also help nominal Christians who do not realize all that Christianity implies.

No one has the monopoly of the Holy Spirit. Let us always remember that we have to receive his gift in all humility (we are not better or greater than anyone else), and that the charisms are of no account unless they are placed at the service of brotherly love. He who has no love and humility cannot advance on the Lord's path, not even by one step. I invite you all to live under the action of the Spirit and, at the same time, to let yourselves be led by him to the very heart of the world, to the heart of men's problems. You have to pray and to act at one and the same time.

Help those who are convinced that the situation of our oppressed, crushed brothers, reduced as they are to a subhuman condition, is so terrible that they must be instantly enabled to live in human conditions and that since their evangelization would take up valuable time, it can always be postponed until later. We have to help them to understand that evangelization and humanization always go hand in hand, by living both aspects of the one gospel simultaneously.

We are discovering with astonishment that the Holy Spirit can act powerfully in the hearts of the poor, crushed by hunger and squalid deprivation. In those areas of destitution where the situation is most subhuman, one finds not submen, not empty-headed human creatures incapable of thinking, but men with ideas, capable of reflecting and open to the Lord's inspiration. This, too, is a surprise of the Holy Spirit.

When in those areas of subhuman poverty one reads a page of the gospel, for example, the most profound and beautiful commentary often comes not from the few cultivated people who are present, but from someone whose conditions of existence are such that they could well reduce a person to a subhuman state. At those moments, one cannot help remembering the words of Christ: "I thank you, Father, for hiding these things from the learned and wise and revealing them to little children" (Mt 11:25).

Let me tell you of an episode taken from the everyday life of North-East Brazil. Annunciade, a poor woman who can neither read nor write, had encouraged her neighbors, threatened with expulsion from their home, to offer resistance. She was arrested and taken away in a police-van to be interrogated by a police officer.

The poor, brought before the police, are far more vulnerable than others, since they have no money and no lawyer to defend them.

Annunciade was trembling with fear; beads of cold sweat stood out on her forehead. But in her heart she was speaking to Christ: "Lord, help me, for without your help I'll do worse than St. Peter and Judas. I'll betray you and I'll betray my neighbors."

At that moment, she recalled a saying of Christ which she had learnt from the animators of Encounter of Brothers, our movement for the evangelization of the people. She remembered that Christ had said: "When they hand you over, do not worry about how to speak or what to say; the Spirit of your Father will be speaking in you" (Mt 10:19–20). These words were so prominent in her mind that she got through the interrogation with great calm.

Released by the police, Annunciade told us that she had given such fine answers that she could not even repeat them. Here we have a close-up of the Holy Spirit's action, in accordance with the Lord Jesus' promise.

Charismatics, my brothers! You who love to pray and to listen to the Lord, stay awake and alert, as he so clearly stresses we should in the gospel,

- —so that you may never use prayer as a pretext for neglecting social and apostolic action;
- —so that you may not criticize those who, without forgetting eternity, remind us that eternity begins here and now and are endeavoring to build up a more just and human world, the kingdom on earth;
- —so that you will refuse to classify Christians simplistically, according to the labels "horizontalist" and "verticalist" which people try to attach to them;
- —so that you do not allow your Christian brothers to be persecuted and treated as subversive agents and Communists simply because they are uniting not in order to trample on the rights of others, but to prevent others from trampling on their own rights.

And more positively:

- —Strive to understand and help those around you to understand, in these times of generalized violence, that the most glaring violence of all is, in fact, the "institutionalized" destitution which prevails throughout the Third World.
- —Strive to discover and help others to discover the bleak areas of destitution right in the middle of the affluent countries.
- —Strive to understand and help others to understand that the only effective way of avoiding armed violence

is to encourage and practice active, courageous non-violence and to exert liberating moral pressures.

— Help to denounce and combat — always peacefully but courageously — the arms race, and particularly the proliferation of nuclear weapons.

— Help to denounce the idolatry of national security, which some governments present as the supreme value, superseding all other values: no genuine democracy can coexist with this idolatry which holds that the end justifies such means as kidnapping, torture and assassination.

— Do everything you can to encourage, personally and actively, the studies and researches which are giving the world a clear view of the unjust structures about which it knows so little; do this in the knowledge that, without this clear vision, the liberating moral pressures will remain superficial and ineffective.

— Draw your strength from the renewal in the Spirit, so that you may help the Church increasingly to overcome its triumphalist temptations and to be unsparing in its efforts to become a living presence of Christ at the service of men and of God's glory.

— Help those Christians whose conflicting tendencies have become polarized to understand that prayer and Christian commitment are intimately united, that a horizontal arm does not of itself form a cross, that a vertical arm does not of itself form a cross, but that both arms extended together form the cross of Christ, embracing both God and mankind in his love!

Charismatics, my brothers! Let us show the world together that the true love of God is so abundant that it must overflow into love of neighbor.

Let us live together the mystery of Pentecost, which was and ever remains a mystery of profound transformation, turning the timorous into courageous apostles, faithful to the point of martyrdom.

And let us pray together to Our Lady of the Magnificat.

Our Lady, teach us to listen
to the Lord's word
with perfect readiness of heart,
in all circumstances,
and to sing with you
the Magnificat that exalts the poor,
with no bitterness,
but with such fullness of love
that if this song wounds anyone,
it leaves only a benign wound
with its own power to heal.

Prayer for Our Brothers, the Rich

Extending Our Lady's Magnificat, I would like to pray for the rich. "Why?," you may ask, "they already possess so many things: money, learning, power. Aren't these sufficient advantages? They surely don't need help!" To which I reply, "all the same, let us pray for them!"

Lord, you alone hold
life, knowledge, freedom.
You alone
possess the true wealth
which cannot be devalued
and remains beyond the grave,
the wealth men share
without becoming poorer.

Grant that our brothers, the rich,
may understand that gold

has no money-power in the Beyond;
that in the land of eternity
love alone is accepted
as authentic currency.

Grant that their too-favored children
may discover the plight of the poor
and not shirk their social duty.
May they not be corrupted by ease
but learn the value of sacrifice
so that a better world may dawn
not against but for them.

NOTES

1. Pastor Thomas Roberts. Quoted from the review *Tychique*, September 1976, p.17
2. G. Gusdorf, *La Parole*, 1963, p. 77.
3. *A New Pentecost?*, Chapter 8: "The Holy Spirit and New Communities," pp. 131–150. The passage by Stephen Clark is quoted on p. 131 and comes from his book: *Building Christian Communities, Strategy for Renewing the Church*, Notre Dame, Ave Maria 1972, pp. 33, 40, 43.
4. Gustavo Gutierrez, *A Theology of Liberation*, London, SCM Press, 1974, p. 177.
5. *Ibid.*, p. 37.

IN THE HEART
OF THE CITY

Cardinal Suenens

Faith and Global Structures

Our existence unfolds within global structures. In simple terms, this means the whole political apparatus, the entire economic order, the overall cultural institution and the general judicial administration of a country, regardless of the name given to its political regime. These global structures result from the organic institutionalization of the norms, roles and collectivities which characterize a system. Has faith anything to say when it is confronted by a global structure? Can it affect a system and its components? If so, how does it affect them? This is the question we must now examine. It is as old as Christianity, but it remains ever-topical.

Among Christians there are at present two conflicting tendencies. The so-called "conservative" tendency wishes the Church to be neutral in socio-political matters, to remain above the fray, and not to adduce the gospel in support of a too categorical option. It wishes the Church to confine itself to purely religious matters, to convert individuals to Christ so that they may subsequently assume their temporal responsibilities as any good Christian should.

The so-called "progressive" tendency, on the other hand,

regards human advancement and cultural, economic and political liberation as an integral dimension of evangelization — indeed, some would say its primordial dimension. It holds that the Church, as the interpreter of Christ's judgment on the world, cannot renounce its critical function and must therefore challenge every form of "established *dis*order."

In the view of the "progressives," such criticism cannot remain superficial, merely denouncing wrongs verbally. It must get down to the root of those evils, in other words, it must radically review the structures that engender the evil.

Hence they conclude that, out of its fidelity to God and Jesus Christ, the Church is duty-bound to go out to the world, to be present and active wherever injustice and human suffering reign, and to contribute with all its might to the healing of society. In any case, they add, in one way or another the Church is obliged to bear witness, willingly or otherwise, as much through its action as through its passivity. So whatever it does, it cannot evade the issue. Let it therefore draw its inspiration from its founder: Jesus Christ, the Head of the Church, who loved and helped the poor, opposed injustice, healed the physical and moral wounds of those whom he encountered on his path. And at this moment he is calling his Church — his Body — to carry on his work and to witness to his love amidst the tensions of society. What attitude must be ours, as Christians?

Let us take the case of the cultural system, which, at first sight, is more closely related to our Christian doctrinal heritage.

The cultural system exercises a considerable and profound ascendancy over the collectivity — over us. In fact, it represents the rules, norms, and patterns which inspire our judgments and actions. It is with reference to this system that we and others judge our conduct to be significant and coherent.

These patterns of culture constitute a real indoctrination, omnipresent and at times constraining, which thoroughly penetrates us.

When the system is institutionalized and thus becomes a structure, it acquires by that very fact the power and weight of an institution.

Mutatis mutandis, the significance of the economic system can be explained in the same way. And that is why the establishment of a "new international economic order" is a topic much discussed by Christians today.

And the same holds true of the political apparatus — hence the recent studies revealing the domination mechanisms inherent in the theory of "national security."

Let us unhesitatingly recognize that there are cultural, economic, and social imbalances which are in urgent need of readjustments, and that this can only be achieved by combined efforts. Problems that far exceed the powers of the individual cannot be solved by personal initiatives alone. The communal life entails specific requirements and obeys its own laws.

We cannot disregard the fact that the transition from the individual to the collective plane introduces a change of scale and hence a change in the nature of human relationships. A society is not just the sum total of its members. It obeys specific laws due to the stability of its institutions, to the richness of a powerful continuity, but also to the passivity of the body of people, to the gregarious instinct and to a law of inertia.

There are certain structural rules of the game which it would be both naive and harmful to overlook.

But, in addition to this, the individual must know how to commit himself as an individual, and if he urges reforms, he must be ready to pay the price for them.

As Didier Aubier, the spokesman of the *Spiritualité et Politique* group has so rightly pointed out:

How, indeed, can we ensure, at one and the same time, more social justice, the protection of nature and the environment, the safeguarding of rare resources, the improvement of working conditions and increased aid to the Third World, without levying a substantial tax on consumer goods in proportion to their non-essential character? Do we really believe that growth in production will be sufficient for coping with these new duties when, at the same time, voters are trying to obtain by law a decrease in the weekly number of working hours, an earlier age of retirement and an extension of the school-leaving age; and when the investments to be realized if we are to ensure this productivity will themselves necessitate stringent economy and savings?

We close our eyes tight so that we may not see this urgent need for changes. And the whole political class tacitly agrees to bury its head in the sand, without realizing that inflation is to a considerable degree the inevitable counterpart of the sacrifices we have failed to impose on ourselves and of the efforts we have been unwilling to make, and that we are thus led to suffer it blindly and in less favorable conditions.

From this viewpoint, it is right and useful to state plainly that the rediscovery and, above all, the application of the gospel values of sharing are indispensable to today's society.[1]

Formerly, poverty was accepted as an unavoidable fact, a fatal historical accident which the Christian endeavored to put right through the numerous initiatives of charity. The human sciences have gradually elicited the causes of poverty; by laying bare the blemishes and injustices of poverty, they have, so to speak, "defatalized" the social inequalities of the economic systems that used to oppress man. This explains the immense effort to rectify the various forms of injustice and to liberate man from the alienations inherent in poverty and, *a fortiori*, in destitution.

From this day forth the proclamation of the gospel permanently includes, for each and every Christian, the duty to contribute personally to that collective and essential righting of social injustices. Today the love of the poor is taking on a socio-political dimension which could not be even remotely apprehended by our ancestors.

Presence and Voice of the Church

For many centuries the Church devoted itself to urgent social needs and ministered to them in the place of the state. Thus it founded schools, hospitals, orphanages and the like, in its desire to relieve immediate want.

At present, as I have just pointed out, there is an ever-growing awareness that it is equally necessary to get down to the root of the evils which the social sciences are increasingly bringing to light. In addition to the "short-range" relations established by love and concern for the immediate neighbor and his most pressing needs, society has turned its attention to "long-range" relations. We now understand much better than our forefathers how deeply the cultural and economic-political framework determines man's concrete living conditions. The emphasis has shifted, but the two concerns are complementary.

The impact of Christians on the world would be immense if they managed to unite their efforts, first of all among themselves, then with all men of good will. How can one fail to subscribe to the following lines by a Protestant theologian, Professor C.H. Pinnock of the Theological Faculty of Hamilton, Ontario? Discussing the charismatic renewal and its social implications, he writes: "If charismatic and evangelical Christians together were committed to the righteousness of the kingdom of God, as they ought to be, in

the context of the societies where they have been called,
they would represent a more radical and redemptive force
than any revolutionary group in existence. The dynamism is
there. What is needed is wise pastoral direction and
encouragement."[2]

Echoing this sentiment, Mgr. Jadot, Apostolic Delegate to
the United States, recently declared: "The goal of the
Charismatic Renewal includes the re-evaluation of the charisms, but extends to the whole of the Christian life in all of
its family, social and cultural implications. This wider
vision of the Charismatic Renewal, as the total transformation of human life and culture according to the demands of
the Gospel, gives hope."[3]

The official and repeated teaching of the Church urges
Christians to assume their responsibilities in the sphere of
social institutions and global structures.

Here I must mention, as particularly important declarations, that of the 1971 Synod of Bishops, held in Rome, and
those of Pope John Paul II and the Latin American Conference of Bishops at Puebla in February 1979.

The 1971 Episcopal Synod, as we know, devoted much of
its attention to the problem of "Justice in the World." It
alluded to "the international systems of domination," and
also to "the objective obstacles which social structures place
in the way of conversion of hearts" (chap.1). Approaching
the question of "international action," the Synod urged
Catholics to give careful consideration to a series of proposi-
tions, of which the following are especially noteworthy:
"Let recognition be given to the fact that international order
is rooted in the unalienable rights and dignity of the human
being"; "Let the United Nations and international organiza-
tions be supported, insofar as they are the beginning of a
system capable of restraining the armaments race"; Let
certain aims be fostered "as first guidelines... for an
economic and social plan for the entire world."

The texts of the Puebla Conference are particularly significant in this respect. The following passage from the *Conclusions* is particularly relevant to our topic:

The Church — speaking generally and without distinguishing the functions incumbent on its diverse members — interprets it as a duty and a right to be present in this sector of life, because Christianity must evangelize the whole of man's existence, including the political dimension. For this reason, it criticizes all those who seek to reduce the area of faith to personal and family life, excluding the professional, economic, social and political orders, as though sin, love, prayer and forgiveness were irrelevant to these spheres.

Truly, the necessity of this presence of the Church in the political realm stems from the inmost depths of the Christian faith: the sovereignty of Christ which encompasses the whole of life. It is Christ who ultimately ensures all human brotherhood whereby one man has the same worth as another: "You are all one in Jesus Christ."

From Christ's integral message flow a wholly new anthropology and theology which embrace man's concrete life, both personal and social (Evangelii Nuntiandi 29). It is a liberating message because it saves man from the bondage of sin, the root and source of all oppression, injustice and discrimination.

These are the reasons for the Church's presence in the political domain, that it might enlighten consciences and proclaim a word capable of transforming society.

Politics, understood in its widest and highest sense, looks to the common good, on both the national and the international scales.

In this broad sense, politics also involves the Church, and therefore its Pastors, the ministers of unity. It is a way of giving worship to the one God, desacralizing the world and at the same time consecrating it to Him.[4]

Theology and Liberating Salvation

The immense and crucial problem presented to our time by the situation of underdevelopment, which is affecting three-quarters of the human race has made our contemporaries increasingly conscious of the reality of the social and collective sin underlying this imbalance. There is now a clearer awareness that sin is not only a personal fault, but that it affects our responsibilities in the cultural, economic, and political domain.

There are sinful structures from which we have to break away, because they institutionalize evil — in other words, selfishness, injustice, oppression and flagrant inequalities — and because they water down the meaning of responsibility and guilt.

This growth of awareness has led Christian groups to re-read the gospel in the light of man's liberation and of our duty to fight against all alienations which reduce him to a subhuman condition — the duty of social and political justice which we must carry out because of our faith in God, the Father of all men, and of our faith in Jesus Christ, the brother and common friend of every human being.

Christ liberated us from sin by redeeming us, from fatalism by awakening us to our responsibilities, and from endless suffering, from death as the world's ultimate "absurdity."

The gospel is the message of salvation and liberation. We have to acknowledge both its spiritual breadth and its logic: that of the Incarnation. As George Bernanos points out, "it is God who is expecting what men expect of us," and this reminder is equally applicable to our socio-political duties.

Over the past few years, a theology "of liberation" has

sprung up in Latin America: it has endeavored to reread scripture through the prism of the poor and the oppressed, bearing in mind the social context of a population that barely manages to survive.

It has strongly underlined the imperative duty of justice for all, as an integral part of God's plan for mankind and the essential prerequisite of peace on earth. It has emphasized the collective and social sin of institutionalized injustice. It has actualized the Old Testament prophets: Isaiah, Amos, Jeremiah, transposing to our time their cries of protest. It has reacted, in the name of the gospel, against the social imbalances within a nation and in the mutual relationships of a people.

This theology obliges all of us to rethink the problem of the close connection between the effort to liberate men and Christian salvation.[5] The question cannot be evaded: what is the relation between social liberation and the liberation—the salvation—brought to us by Jesus Christ?

Neither Identical Nor Separate

Let us speak to the point: earthly salvation cannot be equated with the mystery of salvation which reconciles man with God and liberates him from sin and the finality of death. We cannot attribute a temporal messianism to Jesus. He insistently repeated that his kingdom was not of this world.

But we would be overlooking the meaning of Jesus' earthly action if we forgot that he inaugurated and anticipated here below and in his person the coming kingdom of God. That kingdom is not only a mystical and future reality, it is an all-embracing present reality; it concerns man in all his spiritual and physical dimensions, considered both individually and collectively.

A glimpse of that kingdom was given to mankind when

Jesus worked miracles. In these we discover signs and a kind of foreshadowing of the new world to come, "the new earth and the new heaven."

Christianity cannot be relegated to the purely spiritual and religious without minimizing the scope of Christ's saving Incarnation.

To object that Christ himself was never involved in politics would be to forget that if he was not a social agitator, he nonetheless set in motion, for all future times, the dynamism of a brotherly love which far exceeds the exigencies of purely human solidarity.

Out of fidelity to the Master, the modern Christian, who lives in another social context than the Christian of the first century, must translate the exigencies of Christianity anew, for this time.

Liberation, an All-Encompassing Process

The liberation theologians readily — and fittingly — take situations of economic or political injustice as their starting point. This procedure undoubtedly allows the action of Christians to unfold in a concrete and well-defined situation. But it also limits the field of Christian liberation from the outset. "We can say," writes the South American theologian Gustavo Gutierrez, "that the historical, political liberating event *is* the growth of the Kingdom and *is* a salvific event; but it is not *the* coming of the Kingdom, not *all* of salvation."[6]

Moreover, Gutierrez distinguishes, with exemplary clarity, "three levels of meaning: political liberation, the liberation of man throughout history, liberation from sin and admission to communion with God ... These levels mutually affect each other, but they are not the same. One is not present without the others, but they are distinct: they are all part of a single, all-encompassing salvific process, but they are to be found at different levels" (p. 176).

The salvific process is indeed all-encompassing; and that is why, although each Christian and each Christian group cannot take upon themselves all the initiatives required by the liberation process in its totality, they can nonetheless devote themselves, in accordance with their particular charisms, to a determined task within the overall work of liberation; but without ever depreciating the other functions and projects.

No, nothing escapes the total, all-embracing power of the salvific process. "Nothing," pursues Gutierrez, "is outside the pale of the action of Christ and the gift of the Spirit. This gives human history its profound unity. Those who reduce the work of salvation are indeed those who limit it to the strictly 'religious' sphere and are not aware of the universality of the process" (p. 177).

But there is good evidence that the work of salvation is limited in this way at each stage of the process. Then there is the opposite kind of limitation. From a European and no longer specifically Latin American standpoint, it would also be true to say that when Christian groups of our continent strive for an authentic political or economic liberation, but associate their endeavor with a materialistic anthropology or consider that religious values are irrelevant to the work in hand, they are not fulfilling a completely "Christian" task either, for they are depriving their action of certain features — and not the least important — of the authenticity established by Jesus himself.

The Message of "Gaudium et Spes"

Earthly progress is one thing, the establishment of the kingdom of God is another! They cannot be equated, but they are not wholly distinct from one another. In the Constitution *Gaudium et Spes*, Vatican Council II has very perceptively emphasized their interconnection:

> While we are warned that it profits a man nothing if he gain the whole world and lose himself, the expectation of a new earth must not weaken but rather stimulate our concern for cultivating this one. For here grows the body of a new human family, a body which even now is able to give some kind of foreshadowing of the new age.
>
> Earthly progress must be carefully distinguished from the growth of Christ's kingdom. Nevertheless, to the extent that the former can contribute to the better ordering of human society, it is of vital concern to the kingdom of God.
>
> For after we have obeyed the Lord, and in his Spirit nurtured on earth the values of human dignity, brotherhood and freedom, and indeed all the good fruits of our nature and enterprise, we will find them again, but freed of stain, burnished and transfigured. This will be so when Christ hands over to the Father a kingdom eternal and universal: "a kingdom of truth and life, of holiness and grace, of justice, love, and peace." On this earth that kingdom is already present in mystery. When the Lord returns, it will be brought into full flower (no. 39, 2–3).

The Spirit Who Renews the Face of the Earth

Such is the message of the Church. Could it be said with more insight and authority that full human liberation is fundamentally the work of grace and a gift of God?

The Church places a bold prayer on our lips: "Send forth thy Spirit and they shall be created. And thou shalt renew the face of the earth."

In the heart of the People of God, it is the Spirit who

works the "already accomplished" and prepares the "not yet" of the Kingdom.

It is he who reaches down to man's inmost depths, including all his attachments, and leads him towards the final and total flowering of his existence.

He remains, forever, the creative and renewing Spirit at work in the heart of the world.

By welcoming the Spirit in faith, on the morning of the Annunciation, Mary made possible the mystery of the Incarnation, the starting point of our salvation.

By opening himself to the Spirit, in faith, the Christian will hasten, even now on earth, the coming of the new times.

Prayer

Send your Spirit

Send your Spirit
and all will be created
and you will renew
the face of the earth.

The Spirit who re-creates us

Send your Spirit
first of all,
with priority,
to create me anew,
all of me.
Set me free from my sins,
my fears,
my complexes,
and fill me
to overflowing
with your wisdom,

your power,
your life.

The Spirit who reveals the Father

Send your Spirit
who searches out and reveals
your unfathomable *Father*-tenderness
for all your sons,
whether prodigal or not.
May He teach us to recognize your voice
and to tune in to it
without interference
on your own wave-length.
May He teach us to pray,
calling You by the name of Father,
with the heart of a child
who knows that he is loved and understood.

The Spirit who reveals the Son

Send your Spirit
who reveals the secret of your *Son*,
"in whom you place all your joy"
and in whom we place
all our hope.
May He lead us to understand the gospel,
verse by verse,
in its burning reality.
And may He help us so to translate it
at the heart of the world
that when men see how Christians live
they may recognize in them
the light of his face,
the tone of his voice,

the compassion of his heart
and the tenderness of his smile.

The Spirit who reveals the Church

Send your Spirit
that He may also reveal to us
the true face of your *Church*
beyond the shortcomings of his disciples
who walk with a heavy step,
weighed down by twenty centuries of history.
May He draw us
into the hidden mystery of the Church,
of which Mary is the living Icon,
and may He abide with us
so that your Church may remain,
for each passing generation,
the faithful witness,
the true interpreter,
the sacrament of Jesus.

The Spirit who restores unity

Send your Spirit
on your *divided Church*
in its painful quest
for visible unity;
that your disciples may quicken their step
to hasten the hour
when Love and Truth
will be but one
in the home of your reconciled children;
so that the scandal
which has lasted all too long
may come to an end

and that the world may believe
in Him whom You have sent.

The Spirit who reconciles

Send your Spirit
upon this *world of men*
so that He may win the victory
over their oppositions
and liberate them
from the hatred
and injustice
which tear them apart;
so as to create among them
that brotherly communion
which they gropingly seek,
and which springs from
the sovereign communion
of the Father, and of the Son,
and of the Spirit.
Amen.

NOTES

1. *La Croix*, 29 April 1977, p. 2.
2. Quoted in Cardinal L.J. Suenens: *Ecumenism and Charismatic Renewal*, p. 92, no. 72.
3. Interview with Mgr. Jadot on the Charismatic Renewal in *Logos Journal*, July-August 1978.
4. *The Present and Future of Evangelization in Latin America* (Conclusions of the Puebla Conference, nos. 381, 382, 385).
5. On this subject see the enlightening and perceptive article by the Chilean theologian Segundo Galilea, "The Theology of Liberation. A General Survey," in *Lumen Vitae*, Vol. 33 (1978), No. 3, pp. 331–353.
6. G. Gutierrez, *A Theology of Liberation*, SCM Press, 1974, p. 177.